THE 100 TOP PSYCHICS & ASTROLOGERS IN AMERICA - 2014

BY
PAULETTE COOPER & PAUL NOBLE

Polo Publishing of Palm Beach
with
Green Dragon Books

www.100psychics.com
www.polopublishing.com
www.greendragonbooks.com
www.paulettecooper.com
www.paulnoble.com
www.facebook.com/top100psychicsinamerica
www.twitter.com/top100psychics

Polo Publishing of Palm Beach
Post Office Box 621, Palm Beach, FL 33480
paulettecooper.com, 100psychics.com

with Green Dragon Books
12 South Dixie Highway, Lake Worth, FL 33460
www.greendragonbooks.com

DEDICATION: *To Ted Cooper, an angel*

ISBN: 978-0-9914013-0-7

Internal Design by Dennis & Hilary Ferrand, Chris Campbell
Cover Concept by Dennis Ferrand (frottdesigns@gmail.com)
"Eye" photo by Art Calin
Photos of Paulette Cooper (Noble) & Paul Noble, courtesy of Tina Valant

Made in the United States of America

THE 100 TOP PSYCHICS & ASTROLOGERS IN AMERICA - 2014

THEIR STORIES, SPECIALTIES, AND HOW TO CONTACT THEM

BY
PAULETTE COOPER & PAUL NOBLE

INTRODUCTION

THE PSYCHICS AND ASTROLOGERS IN THIS BOOK ARE CONSIDERED TO BE THE BEST IN AMERICA TODAY....

AND NO MATTER WHERE YOU LIVE, YOU CAN CONTACT THEM FOR A PHONE (OR IN-PERSON) READING

You are about to read the fascinating personal stories of America's top psychics and astrologers. They "speak" in their own words, so you can learn who they are, how they discovered their gifts, how they became successful, and what they do for their clients — which could include you. With this book, it's easy to see how to contact them by phone or e-mail. But even if you don't want a session, just reading their stories is fascinating.

Some specialize in sex, love, crime, dogs, cats, horses, Oscars, travel, real estate, business, shopping, fashion, healing—and helping people with everything from life options to stock options, and more. Some use Feng Shui, or Reiki, tarot, automatic writing, numerology, and more; some are guided by angels, some by spirits, and some by others.

Many of them have become famous; and/or channeled the famous, and/or read for the famous. Some are psychics or intuitives (pretty much the same thing); others are mediums who try to reach those who have passed on; several are astrologers; and many are combinations of these. Included also are interviews with a numerologist and a palmist.

The 58 people with full interviews (42 more are listed in the back) are the most checked out, vetted list of psychics and astrologers anywhere. Those who want a reading and have this book no longer have to choose someone from an advertisement, or from a so-called "best" list on the Internet (where people paid to be included), or by calling a psychic hotline, or stopping at a gypsy storefront psychic on the street.

Now, you can learn all about the top people in the metaphysical field right here. Most of these included have been sufficiently accurate and/or helpful that their clients have continued to return—and recommend them. They've built up successful practices based on repeat businesses and word-of-mouth— unlike those who depend on people's impulses to call a stranger or pop in a shop.

Most of the people included in this book were also chosen by major media. We started our search for the top by selecting people who had already been sufficiently successful to appear on major shows (*Oprah, Dr. Phil, Dr. Oz*, etc.), or in major publications *(The New York Times, The Los Angeles Times, The Wall*

Street Journal, etc.), or had won impressive awards (Lifetime TV's *Psychic Challenge* show) or special recognition (by a columnist for a major newspaper).

No other group of psychics and astrologers has ever been as thoroughly researched. We spent months going through thousands of websites, newspapers and magazine articles, radio programs, books, videos, YouTube and more. We discarded hotline phone psychics (or phone-y psychics) and storefront psychics. Instead, we focused on people who pleased enough clients to get full time work, mostly on word of mouth or top media exposure.

After choosing the ones who seemed promising, we Googled them (well past the first page), reviewed them elsewhere online, and even criminally checked some to see if they had ever been arrested or were using aliases.

The hand-chosen few who remained then answered an extensive questionnaire, and were given follow-up phone calls, e-mail questions, and even personal visits. No one paid to be in this book or its website.

Those who survived this rigorous and impartial selection process—and had interesting stories to tell—are included here with full interviews. In the back of the book are more of America's top psychics and astrologers, with their specialties and how to contact them. Many were recommended by others in this book, but there was not enough time or space to interview them; that may be saved for the next book.

We hope that if you contact anyone in this book for a reading, that you will have the kind of favorable experiences many others have had with them. But we are not recommending any one here. We are just sharing with you which interesting psychics/astrologers are considered to be the tops in their areas of expertise.

As you read on a number of these websites, a visit to a psychic or astrologer is for entertainment purposes only. If you have a reading, it's not a substitute for treatment from a licensed professional. Any readings of any people you may have learned of through this book provides no guarantees or implied warranties, and we will not be held accountable for any interpretations or decisions made or actions taken based on information provided by people in this book.

Paulette Cooper & Paul Noble
PauletteAndPaul@aol.com
PO BOX 621
PALM BEACH, FL 33480

TABLE OF CONTENTS

INTUITIVE ASTROLOGER

SHELLEY ACKERMAN

Shelley@KarmicRelief.com
(212) 539-3100

www.KarmicRelief.com

An extremely successful cabaret singer, this intuitive astrologer and counselor shines as brightly in her second career.

www.facebook.com/KarmicRelief
www.linkedin.com/pub/shelley-ackerman/5/102/b2
www.twitter.com/KarmicRelief

For a phone or in-person reading, call (212) 539-3100 or email
Shelley@KarmicRelief.com

What case makes you still smile remembering it? One woman brought her ten-year-old son to me while she remained for the duration of the session. At the end of the consult, the young boy turned to his mother and said, "This was a lot more fun than that dumb psychiatrist you take me to."

Your Wikipedia entry is very impressive. Care to summarize? They list many movies and shows I've been in, as well as where I got my start, which was as a singing-waitress at Manhattan's famed Improv comedy club. I've also performed in major cities and venues from the Playboy Club to the Continental Baths. My intuitive abilities probably played more of a role than I realized at the time. In 1990, I won *Backstage* magazine's "Bistro Award" for Best Vocalist in New York City. And, oh yes, I sang for many years at the popular spot Catch a Rising Star. I guess I took the club's name literally!

Did you meet many celebrities? About a year after graduating at the age of 16—I skipped a year—I began working at the Improv and met and worked closely with many of the comics who have dominated TV in the past three to four decades—Jay Leno, Bill Maher, Billy Crystal, Elayne Boosler, David Brenner, Larry David, Robert Klein, and Richard Belzer. Richard lived with me for more than a year and we almost married. I've also collected birth information from many other well-known people—including Bill Clinton's from his mother, Virginia, who gave me his exact birth time.

How did your work with these celebrities help you decide on your late career? Born of an early interest, I intuitively began collecting accurate birth data on them in between shows, read it to them, and they were astounded. Now I tell my clients, pay attention to the hobbies that most interest you as they may morph into careers later on.

What non-celeb do you think you helped the most? A woman came to me in 1998 or 1999. She was working for a financial company in the World Trade Center. She was working on commission and they were advancing her a pittance. We went back and forth as to why another situation would be better. Finally, exasperated I said, "I want you out of that building!"

Did you hear back from her after 9/11? In September 2002, I was on a radio show commemorating the one year anniversary of 9/11. That same woman called in and told me she was in Building 2 on that fateful morning. After the announcement came over the speakers saying "We have secured the building—

stay at your desks," she heard my utterance ("I want you out of that building!") go through her head. She grabbed her belongings and began running down the stairs. About 20 minutes later, the second airplane hit the building. She was on the lower floors of the staircase but made it out
to survive and tell the tale.

How atypical was your background? I am the daughter of an orthodox rabbi and a glam professional singer. I was raised on New York's Lower East Side, and attended a parochial day school—half a day English, half Hebrew. I graduated from The High School of Music and Art at 16. The movie *Fame* was eerily autobiographical. I was "over-sensitive" and daydreamed as a child, and though I was a good student, I never quite fit in. How I wish astrology was there for me to help me back then.

What type of charts do you enjoy working on most? I enjoy selecting electional charts for weddings, the launching of a business or a website, and very specific charts to travel on. I specialize in vocational, relationship, motivational, and "creative" applications of astrology.

What type of writing do you do? I write regularly for a cultural magazine called *TheAesthete.com*, and have written regularly for *Beliefnet.com*, *The New York Post* and others. In 2006, I appeared in an article on the front page of *The Wall Street Journal*, and when the IAU, the International Astronomical Union, demoted Pluto as a planet, the paper ran my letter: "Whether he's a planet, an asteroid or radio-active matzo ball, Pluto has proven himself worthy of a permanent place in all horoscopes."

When did you first realize you had this gift? I was born with the ability to remember the birthdays of every person I ever met. I can also remember the details of every astrological chart I've ever done. As for my intuitive abilities, I would occasionally "hear" information and "get" certain "knowings" that were unusual and on target, but since I had no reference points or adult guidance to explain these sensations to me, I did not quite know what to do with them. I had a sense that there was some sort of intelligence that I was connected to. Later on, astrology helped enormously in organizing me.

What do you think you do that's different than what others who are in the metaphysical fields do? There is no competition on the spiritual plane.

MEDIUM

GEORGE ANDERSON, JR.

Andrew@GeorgeAnderson.com
(516) 568-1052 Mon. - Thurs. 10-5
www.GeorgeAnderson.com

For his incredible ability to talk to those who have passed over, he has become one of the most famous mediums in America.

www.facebook.com/GeorgeAndersonMedium

BOOKS: "Walking in the Garden of Souls," "Ask George Anderson," "George Anderson's Lessons from the Light," "We Don't Die: George Anderson's Conversations with the Other Side," "Our Children Forever: George Anderson's Message from Children on the Other Side."

To schedule a phone or in-person reading, call (516) 568-1052 or visit georgeanderson.com/programs.htm

What is the difference between personal contact with loved ones and receiving regular messages from someone else? I can only talk about myself and mediumship. I find it easier and more appealing to deal with your great grandfather or your favorite cousin than with somebody who died in the arena with Spartacus.

What are the most touching cases for you? Those involving parents losing children, especially those who have lost them through miscarriages, SIDS, still births or abortions. Society gives these people very little support, and it can also be frustrating for children who have passed over to see their bereaved parents feeling abandoned.

What do you tell these parents? I often have to relay to them from their offspring that it was simply "my time to go." Bereaved parents often say to me afterward, "I feel better knowing my child is not alone. Now I know I can talk to my child whenever I want to. It is a great comfort to know that they will not forget me and that we will all be together soon."

Do some of the departed send you stronger messages than others? There seems to be a connection between tragic, unusual, or very emotional circumstances at passing and the strength and clarity of the spirit's communication. Someone whose passing left loved ones with regret or severe grief seems to make an extra effort to provide solace. In contrast, when we look at a grandparent who quietly passed away at a ripe old age of natural causes, they usually have little to say.

Can you give an example of a case in which someone had an emotional passing and there was a strong communication afterward with the family? A ten-year-old boy named Charles was killed by three other kids slightly older than he was. They approached Charles and demanded he hand over his denim jacket. When he refused, they attacked him and stuffed several cotton bandannas down his throat. He choked to death. The three boys were accused of the murder. The father of one of them requested my help. Through me, Charles sent forgiving vibrations for this man's son, which comforted and relieved the father.

When did you reveal to the world that you could communicate with the departed? After I graduated from high school and college, and got a job for the telephone company, I began doing readings on a local radio show. It was 1980, and I explained to the audience that I could communicate with the hereafter. The departed spoke to me or sent pictures, and I then deciphered their meaning. By 1981, I was co-hosting my own show.

What changed your life when you were young? At six, I got chicken pox. Complications set in, and a virus attacked my central nervous system. I got encephalitis and was paralyzed for two months. I was never the same after I recovered. Suddenly, I could tell people what had happened to them and to those around them in the past—sometimes before I was born.

When did you start sharing your visions with others? Around the same time, I began to be able to see spirits of deceased people. I thought there was nothing unusual about it, and I even told my friend Tommy that his grandmother had black around her and would soon be going over to the other side. His negative reaction to this confused me, and caused me to be more careful. I began revealing my information only to those who I felt believed me.

Who was The Lilac Lady? "The Lilac Lady," as I called her, was a woman in lilac robes who appeared whenever I was a little down. In school, I occasionally spoke of these spirits and my visions, and the nuns began worrying and keeping an eye on me. My fellow classmates taunted me. One day, a bully was trying to stuff me into a locker. I said, "I see that your father is a drunk and beats up on you and your mother every night." After that, the students became afraid of me and shied away. I became a loner.

Did your visions lead others to misunderstand you? As the visions became stronger, I confided about them to a nun. She told my parents. The school authorities thought I was about to have a nervous breakdown, and they even sent me to a mental health center for testing. And then, a psychiatrist wrongly diagnosed me as a passive schizophrenic!

What type of state are you in during your readings? Experts have monitored my physical responses with an electrocardiograph to measure my heart rate and an electroencephalograph to measure my brain wave activity. My brain waves alternate between alpha, a state of deep relaxation and passive awareness, to beta, an alert, physically active state. My heart rate increases from the normal 70 beats per minute to 113 or 114 during a trance state.

PSYCHIC

FRANK ANDREWS

261 Mulberry Street
New York, NY 10012

(212) 226-2194

He is sometimes called the Rolls-Royce of psychics because over the span of 52 years he has read for John Lennon, Yoko Ono, Grace Kelly, Christina Ford, Jason Alexander and Perry Ellis, among others.

To schedule an in-person reading, call
(212) 226-2194

Did you and John Lennon hit it off? We did and we didn't. See, if they don't like what I have to say, they get very upset. They want to hear that it's all going to be wonderful and everything is going to be roses. I don't blame them, but I can't do that unless that's the way it is. So what I try to do is find a way to make it wonderful and to make it roses.

What kind of questions did John ask? "Will the Beatles get together again?" "No," I told him, "but I see them on Broadway." Of course, we later had *Beatlemania*. I also suggested to John that he was troubled by his homosexuality. "Why do you dress Yoko up as a boy?" I asked him. He was furious. I also read his palm and found signs of conflict and madness.

How did you end up as Yoko's reader? Although John was a little upset about some of the things I had to say, he told me once that I was very clever. But after I had been reading him mostly, he said, "You know everyone wants to know me. Why don't you know Yoko? She's the one who needs a friend. Why don't you be Yoko's friend?" So I worked with her for about ten years.

Did you foresee John's murder? I told John and Yoko that John would have a tragic ending and die sleeping in blood at an early age.

What about your experience with Princess Grace of Monaco? The first time I read for her I said, "Would you like to hear this as the princess or as Grace?" She smiled and kissed me on the cheek and said, "Honey, tell me like it is!" So I just went to town and let her have it.

What was the most significant thing you told her? That she should leave her husband, get out of Monaco, go back to Hollywood, and start acting again. She asked me once "Do you feel I'm going to die in a car?" I said she would have a heart attack or stroke while driving. She said she wanted me to come to Monaco, but I never saw her after that.

Did she tell people she had seen you? When she was on *Entertainment Tonight*, she said she met the famous psychic Frank Andrews. I thought that was so funny, her being who she was. And then she said, "He said I should go back to Hollywood and act." She had just started getting back into it when she died.

Have you worked with other famous people? Many. When William Shatner interviewed my client, Jason Alexander, he said how I predicted the name of the doctor that was able to help his wife get pregnant—and they now have two sons. He claimed the experience with me was like Fellini. I read for Perry Ellis, but when he came to me, he was in marketing, he wasn't a designer. And I saw him as a designer. But when I told him, he laughed at me and thought I was crazy. I told him not to fly to Fire Island.

He canceled the trip, and the plane crashed, killing pilot and the passengers.

Give a non-celebrity example of one of your cases. This guy I was reading for, and the whole reading was about him leaving his wife. I told him I didn't like the girlfriend he was going to run away with. I said to him, "Why don't you give it a month?" He said that his mind was made up, and I said, No it isn't, because if it was, why did you come to see me?"

When I saw him again, he said he had told his girlfriend that something came up and he couldn't leave for a couple of weeks. So she went and married somebody else! "How much could she have loved you if in two weeks she meets a guy and runs off?" I asked him.

Do you wish some people wouldn't call you? I don't like when people become dependent on me. When they don't call, I know they were able to figure it out. It's very rare that anyone calls and says, "Everything is great." "Everything is wonderful." They usually call when there's a crisis.

What was your first prediction? At one point, I was studying pantomime. That's what I really wanted to do in life, and I was studying in a dance class with Michael Bennett. I said to him, "You know, Michael, you're going to be very, very famous one day. I can see you on Broadway." Well, he became known as Mr. Broadway because he did so many big musicals, like *A Chorus Line* and *Dream Girls*. In fact, one of the characters in *A Chorus Line* was patterned after me.

PSYCHIC

AJ BARRERA

info@AJBarrera.com
(310) 889-9888 or (310) 889-0869

www.AJBarrera.com

He is the most famous Mexican-American psychic in America.

www.facebook.com/PsychicMediumAJBarrera
www.twitter.com/AJBarrera

To schedule a phone or in-person reading, call (310) 889-9888 or
e-mail info@ajbarrera.com

What is the Mexican attitude toward divination? With my culture, there is fear of the whole idea of ghosts, spirits, psychics, mediums, because as Catholics, we were taught that what I do is evil. That it's the devil's work or it comes from a negative place. It would be good if our culture would understand that this work comes from good light and good intentions and not from someone who is doing or practicing magic.

Have some people had bad experiences with Mexican psychics? Unfortunately, yes. Many clients of my culture have come to me for a private reading, mentioning bad experiences from a healer or psychic in their culture. The healer or psychic said there was a spell on them, a black cloud is over them, or someone is stuck and they can't cross over. Unfortunately, there are those who are doing this work with wrong intentions.

Has it helped or hurt you in this country to be Mexican-American? Many talk shows, radio shows, like the fact that I come from a different background. They also like the fact that I'm not a 'normal' psychic medium. I'm young guy, who is real, tell-it-like-it-is person when doing this work, likes to have fun but also serious with my work. I was recently joking around that people are looking for something 'spicy' in psychic mediums and apparently I am it.

How did you get started professionally? At 19 years old, I found myself appearing weekly on two popular radio shows in Los Angeles, *Angels In Waiting* on KOST 103.5 & *Radio Medium*, each with between two to four million listeners. I gave validation and healing messages to listeners from their deceased loved ones. From there, I immediately established a large clientele across the world.

Have you ever had a case where someone wished they hadn't come to you? When I was 20 years old, I remember conducting an in-person reading for a gentleman who looked like he could have been in his mid-50's. I immediately connected with his father who was in the spirit world, as well as with a man that he did not want to hear from. The client got into a fight with the now deceased guy on the other side who had just appeared. The client had ended up killing this man in the room and doing some time for it.

How did he react? When the client heard details of how the man had passed away, he immediately jumped off my couch in shock, not wanting to hear or deal with the matter. "I need to leave right now." That moment, I realized that

I may have been too detailed about how it all went down.

Have you had any other careers or interesting jobs before this? I attended a junior college to be a fire fighter or move into law enforcement. I had a retail job for a couple of years while doing my weekly radio appearance in Los Angeles and conducting private readings. I remember reading for so many random people at my work and those who walked in to shop that there was a running joke with many co-workers that anyone who gets hired or buys an item from me get a free reading!

Did your intuitive abilities play a role in this (these) jobs? I would often see colors around people, feel a presence of a deceased loved one or had a feeling that there should be something a person should know. It took me some time to finally really learn how to ground myself through meditation, where I would not pick up information around people.

Is there "medium" work that you find uncomfortable? Personally, I feel the pain or emotion when parents lose their child at a young age. It doesn't matter how they passed way. It could have been medical, an accident or self-inflicted. Those cases are always the hardest because no child should leave before their parent.

Do you feel the media portrays mediumship accurately? I have no objections to my 13-episode reality series *From Beyond* which aired in 2011 on NBC Universal Mun2. But generally I am not a big fan of movies or shows that mock the work of metaphysics. I feel oftentimes that Hollywood puts too much of the spook factor in it, that those who do not know of this work may see it in the eyes of a creator/ producer, which may be negative.

What do you feel you're especially good at? My main forte is mediumship. It's kind of a three way conversation. I connect with my spirit, spirit then gives that information to my spiritual guides, and then they give to me to deliver. I also focus on psychic blockages that an individual may have, which I call, "Intuitive Counseling."

PSYCHIC

COLETTE BARON-REID

www.ColetteBaronReid.com

This well known New Hampshire spiritual intuitive is published in 27 languages and has penned eight best selling books, apps, and cards, and has been featured on Dr. Oz, The Doctors, W, Elle and other major media.

www.facebook.com/cbr.psychic
www.linkedin.com/pub/colette-baron-reid/7/18b/6ab
www.twitter.com/ColetteBR

BOOKS: "The Map: Finding the Magic and Meaning in the Story of Your Life," "Journey Through the Chakras," (CD) "Messages from Spirit," "Remembering the Future," "Weight Loss for People Who Feel Too Much."

When did you first realize you had this gift? I had recurring dreams when I was small, seeing a skeletal man being pushed into a giant oven and seeing gold in a pile on a table beside a pile of teeth. My grandfather was killed in Dachau—but we never knew any of this until I was 25. Apparently it was common for the SS officers to pull the teeth of the ones going to be exterminated and extract the gold to make jewelry. But, I've had numerous experiences of knowing things about others without prior knowledge all my life.

Were you different as a child or did you have an unusual background? I always felt I was different. I felt too much, I knew too much, I couldn't tell where I ended and you began. Took many years to find a balance and be grounded.

How did you get started professionally? I fell into this reluctantly. I was pursuing a career as a singer-songwriter and worked as an aromatherapy massage therapist for my day job. As soon as I started touching people I "remembered" stories about them in my head and began mentioning what I saw.
Within a very short time word of mouth spread and no one wanted to book a massage—just a reading. It was so easy though, and I think when something comes so effortlessly you minimize it, thinking it might not be important.

What troubled you at the beginning? I had a real aversion to the stereotype of the "psychic fortuneteller" and really struggled with what this ability meant. For the first six years I told people "I don't really do this, I'm really a singer" until someone called from India to book an appointment. He heard about me in an airport. Kinda hit me in that moment. Man plans god laughs. Thank god I didn't quit- it is my true mission—to see, guide and advise with my intuitive skill.

What person did you help the most? I think the most poignant experience happened when I was in Nashville for a speaking demonstration (talking and giving readings from the stage) and just before I got on stage I saw images in my mind of a yellow tricycle, and Chinese broccoli—which is called Kai-lan, and an urgent feeling that I was to see someone to tell this to, that this odd combination somehow would bring peace. Before I went onstage I saw a woman and began a conversation with her and told her I was trying to figure out these two things. It was amazing. She had lost her son Kylen to an accident and was seeking closure. She also had a photograph of the little yellow trike. It was so meaningful to bring healing to a mother's broken heart. Especially since mediumship is not my primary skill or focus.

What do you think you do that's different (unique, better) than what other intuitives do? My clients refer to me as "The Oracle"—a nickname that's now stuck and I use it on my website.
I specialize in helping leaders and influencers move forward as an intuitive strategist and coach. It's like I am the one who sees in the dark and around corners, a kind of "risk management" if you will—empowering choices rather than giving absolutes.

What are you especially good at? My skill is seeing patterns in events and in people's emotions- what motivates people, how choices create our reality. It's like I see how everyone's stories intersect like roads on a map. I "see" images in my mind, like I'm remembering someone, what happened to them, where they're now, where they're going, who they've met, their impact on the world. I see someone's mission and purpose, the lessons, their impactful relationships and their meaning. A typical session for me is phone or Phone or Skype-30 minutes, general consultation, or one hour business strategy/ coaching.

Which of your predictions (or astrological charts) was most accurate and why? I think my most accurate predictions were because the person never changed course. The future is not written in stone. Predictions are snapshots of potential and possibility and I'm convinced they can change if someone changes direction.

What types of people come to you? Educated, arts and business professionals, spiritually aware, open minded, curious, excited about life, in transition, needing confirmation, understanding, and /or strategic guidance.

How do you feel about your work? Mediumship happens to me spontaneously on stage when I'm speaking. IT's curious because pets come through so clearly- that's my favorite part and I'm fascinated because of how it happens and how it touches people. It started happening when I began touring with Hay House. I used to be so skeptical, even though I've done this for 23 years I believe stuff only when I see it. I don't really understand it but I am 1000 percent convinced we are more than we know. I love my work I consider myself blessed.

PSYCHIC

VICTORIA BEARDEN

v1bear@aol.com
(760) 634-1028

www.AstrologerVic.com
www.VBearden.com

*Although she uses Astrology with her clients, this artist is also a
Psychic, Tarot Master, Numerologist, Face Reader, Spirit Medium—
and House Clearer.*

www.facebook.com/AstrologerVic
http://www.linkedin.com/pub/victoria-bearden/27/744/796
www.twitter.com/AstrologerVic

To schedule a phone or in-person reading, call (760) 634-1028 or
go to http://www.AstrologerVic.com

How did you become an astrologer and Tarot Master? The minute I understood astrology, I realized I had found a logical way to make sense of things. And I began to look into numerology and other ancient wisdoms. Once I learned how to create a chart, I saw that I could help people with this. So, while I was studying art in college, I began to do private readings to earn pocket money. Tarot also showed me a great tool to explain psychic impressions to people. A lot of things just come to me, and divination with tarot cards gave things a grounding.

Do the messages you get from tarot, astrology and psychic readings interfere with each other or confirm things? For me, there's a seamless use of charts, tarot, the person himself or herself. These methodologies enhance each other and give me extra doorways to explore.

What about face reading? As an artist, [see www.astrologervic.com/art] I can look at a person's face, study it, and it helps me with the reading. I remember one person who came to me. His face was asymmetrical, distorted in many ways, with unusual features. I saw mismatched eyes, ears malformed. I talked with him about his past. I saw a tortured life, difficulties, and yet his face had a humanitarian spirit. It turns out he had been through horrible addictions, years of imprisonment. His career now was to help others.

How do you clean a house of its spirits? I've done many "Energy Clearings" because of negative energy at a location, unwanted spirit activity, and so on. I bring a pendulum, white sage, frankincense/myrrh, and my Tibetan spirit chaser bells. I always walk the property first with my pendulum, and assess the situation, to see what's going on and where energy is "stuck." Often times, I get psychic information about the nature of the difficulty, and what previous occupants or the deceased might have to do with it. Sometimes it's a spirit problem, sometimes it's just an energy block. Then I go through a systematic clearing process in each area where there is a problem, using my own energy to channel higher energies. I check with the pendulum to see if it works, and also check in psychically. The sage, bells, and incense are used on my final walk through of the property, to "seal the energy" and clear any residual gunk that might be hanging around. Sometimes things must be repositioned, fixed, or changed in a home or on the property to destroy negative energy and prevent it from being created.

Do house clearings ever not work? On rare occasion there is a vortex or something going on at a location that is simply "inoperable." In one case, through my psychic investigation, later verified, the property was set on a battleground in the Mexican-American War. After that time, the property had been used to raise livestock, and animals were slaughtered where the house was. When I told the home owners about my visions, they admitted to me that they had been finding animal bones buried around the property everywhere... and had even found some bones they thought might be human!

What do you say if someone's chart indicates the end is near? I am careful if I bring that up. But since death is a part of life, I need to help them know about it. If I tell them they need to see their mother right now, or to find out if their parent's affairs are in order, I have to tell them.

Can you communicate with animals? When I was little, I thought animals were telling me things. I connected with animals. I took it for granted that I could communicate with them. I am fascinated with snakes. I walked up to a boa constrictor in the zoo. It woke up and coiled itself up and looked right at me. A whole crowd was behind me and they were amazed.

Have people with someone close to them who have committed suicide come to you for help? I've done many readings for people who wanted insight, contact, or closure regarding a loved one who took their own life. One woman wanted to know about her brother, who had committed suicide. I immediately saw a large body of water and a man, alone, in a small boat. He was very sad and had a small pistol with him.
Then, I caught a quick glimpse of his face. His eyes were closed and he was smiling and peaceful. I saw that the man felt he needed to leave the earth plane, as he was in too much pain. When I told her about my vision that he was at peace, she felt better. She told me that her brother had taken his small boat out to sea and shot himself.

Did problems arise with your ex-husband because of your profession? Yes, he was keeping serious secrets from me during our marriage. Of course, I figured it out, and he didn't like that one bit. Still, my psychic ability actually probably saved my life and my sanity in that ill-fated marriage.

ASTROLOGER

VIRGINIA BELL

CityStarsNY@yahoo.com

www.VirginiaBellAstrology.com
www.YouAreNeverTooLate.com

Virginia Bell has created astrology columns for several major magazines and websites and blogs for The Huffington Post

To schedule a phone or in-person reading, email
CityStarsNY@yahoo.com.

How can astrology help people? Astrology has taught me that we all bloom at different times. Some of us are late bloomers and slow learners. Who cares? Dreams don't have an expiration date. Astrology is a valuable tool that can help you understand your path in life as well as your individual timing and how best to fulfill it. I've learned that every delay and detour is a necessary part of the process. Ultimately it is the journey of becoming whole.

Did you have a happy childhood? I grew up in a crazy, chaotic and abusive environment; I was lonely and insecure but I had big dreams. At 19 I moved to Rome where I worked as an actress. I traveled all over the world and had lots of adventures but didn't have a clue as to what I really wanted. In my late twenties I returned to New York; it was my Saturn Return and I was ready to get serious.

What is your background? I've always been obsessed with food. So in 1974 I opened one of the first natural foods restaurants in New York City, Whole Wheat 'N Wild Berrys. I worked hard, learned self-respect and grew in ways I never thought possible. The restaurant became a success. I even healed my eating disorder which I had since I was 16.

When did you become an astrologer? In 1988 I opened a second restaurant in Massachusetts but it failed. At the same time someone gave me a book that changed my life, Steven Forrest's *The Inner Sky*. Since 1995 I've been a full time astrologer and writer. I've created astrology columns for magazines and websites such as *US Weekly*, *TV Guide*, and *Refinery29*. I currently write for the CBS magazine (Watch!) and blog for the *Huffington Post*. I've studied with Steven Forrest since 2000. In 2010 I wrote the foreword to his book, The *Book of the Moon*. I'm presently writing a book about the generational cycles; *You Are Never Too Late: Using Astrology to Thrive in the Second Half of Life*.

What advice do you give women to achieve the kind of serenity you have? It does get better as you get older—as long as you keep growing and healing. Don't concentrate on removing the wrinkles and cellulite: work on eliminating the stress, anger, and self-criticism. The fountain of youth is not what you do (or eat) but who you are and how you feel about yourself. Don't compare yourself to others—that's really an act of violence.

Why do you call yourself a sex psychic? I honestly think you always find someone who does what you do better than you. So I ask a higher power than me to bring me the people who need the gifts I have to offer. And to bring me those whom I am the best for. Guess where that led me! To Sex. Ladies would call me up and say "Someone referred me to you because you talk about sex." My question "Doesn't everybody?" But many people just didn't feel comfortable asking just anyone about their personal and private sex lives. So they came to me. Plus people who were having paranormal sex cases began contacting me. I couldn't get away from it if I wanted to or if I tried.

How do you feel about sex? I am very sex positive, and feel if you heal your sexuality, you can heal anything. I personally feel your sexuality is the essence of who you are, and it's how you got to this planet, so there has to be something to this sex stuff, right? This thing that so many want to keep hidden and pretend it doesn't exist. Are we ashamed of who we are? And what are we hiding? Since I have these questions I wanted answered, I guess my guides said "You're the one for the job!"

How can you help people with sexual problems? I've learned that you can talk to body parts, including genitalia; they do have something to say. Just like the liver may speak of heat and anger and the kidneys of fear and frustration, each body part holds different energy. Sometimes it wants something very different than what you are giving it. What do your genitals want? I'm great at talking to those body parts now. As far as I know I am the only one who can do what I do, or does what I do publicly.

Do you believe in sex demons? There are paranormal sex cases, where people are being attacked by spirits or making love to a spirit. Some believe they have sex demons. I come in and communicate with whatever is there, or try to get the person some help if it seems that it's in their head or trauma not associated with spirits.

Did you have a typical childhood? I was raised a Jehovah's Witness. They taught me being psychic was demonic and ghosts were just demons. There was no room for growth or expansion or learning because the rules were strict even though they could be wrong. If you doubted them you doubted God. But I remember sitting in the corner praying and rocking back and forth that the ghost in the house would go away. I experienced them on a regular basis. I don't know if you would call this unusual as it was just my childhood experiences. To me it was a very scary norm. Being at home alone seeing faces in the TV screen when the TV was off and hearing voices. Or I would sit outside waiting for someone to come home.

How did this become your career? At a very young age I remember watching "The Psychic Friends" commercials and wishing I could be a psychic and wishing I had special powers. I sometimes did random free, fun readings but forgot about my gift.

But as I got older that vision faded. I trained at nursing homes but couldn't stand the smell and left an hour into training. I took the test for the post office but a 9-5 didn't sit well with me. I started working in restaurants and bridal shops and I even did temp work. When I went to school for massage and Reiki, my life changed almost instantly! I was more intuitive and everything started shifting... it shifted me right out of this country!

How does your gift affect your private life? Dating is hard, because you know before you know. "Yes, it will work, no it won't work." "He's so cute, but"... Or you meet someone amazing and they say: "Wow, can you read me." That is an instant turn off. Now I feel like your therapist with no chance or potential to be your date.

What kind of people do you find hardest to read? Cynical people and skeptics. If you are there just to disprove no matter what is said, what's the point? In your mind you are already right!

The worst is reading for people who have absolutely nothing going on in their lives now or in the near future, and they still want you to pull the rabbit out of the hat when there is none. I don't like getting cases that are hard or difficult to heal or help. As a person of service you wish everyone could receive instant benefits.

MEDIUM AND MINISTER

RITA BERKOWITZ

SpiritRita@aol.com
(781) 871-2563

www.TheSpiritArtist

*A Massachusetts medium and ordained minister, she is co-author of
"The Complete Idiot's Guide to Communicating with Spirits," and
has also written about what happens when a medium loses someone
close to her.*

To schedule a phone or in-person reading, call
(781) 871-2563 or e-mail spiritrita@aol.com

As a medium who has helped so many others through the transition, how did you feel when it happened in your family? This time it was my mother lying there in the hospital bed getting ready to make her transition. She was the strongest woman I have ever known, and was lying there fragile and small, tiny, and unable to speak.

But didn't you feel that she was going to a better place? I knew about the higher side of life. I knew that she would be going to a better place, free of pain. I was still aware of my abilities to see both sides of life. But being a medium did not take away the pain of loss. That pain is real and the grief should be experienced, but the healing that could happen because I could see her and talk to her has been profound

Did you experience any emotions besides sadness? To be honest, in addition to grief, there was a bit of curiosity of wanting to see what would actually happen as my own loved one, my mother, made her transition to the Higher Side of life. As a medium, I have helped so many people through their process of crossing to the Higher Side or dealing with grief. I have described the experiences of what their loved ones have shown me as they were getting ready to cross, who was there and what was happening. But, this time it was different, it was my mother.

Did you comfort her before she passed over? When I got to the hospice, it was obvious the time was close. I took my mother's hand and started to pray and send healing. I sat there holding her hand. Soon, I saw a white mist leave her body through her mouth and nose. I knew it was time.
I told her I loved her and that when the time was right, that she could go and that all of us would be okay. I wept, giving our mother permission to go the Higher Side.

What happened after she passed over? Maybe an hour later I saw this vision behind my Mom's head. I saw my Father's Spirit. He appeared quite young with a beautiful head of thick golden hair, strapping muscles and a smile on his face.
I could see him take my mother's hand and lead her out. She looked so young also, with longer hair and a radiant smile. And then the image disappeared. It was time for her to join him. I later found a picture of them when they were dating. That is how they looked in the vision.

How had your mother felt about your helping others to pass? When she was here on this earth, she would always say to me, "I don't understand what you do." I would explain that I speak to people who have crossed and give their messages to the people who have been left behind. And I would tell her that when she eventually crossed, I would speak to her. She would laughingly say, "I won't speak to you!" I'd say, "Yes you will, I'm the only one who can hear you." Three weeks later, when I was leading a healing service at our church, she came to me again and said, "Now I understand what you do." I can't even begin to tell you how much those words meant to me. After all this time and after crossing over, she knew and she understood what my life's work is about.

You are best known for "spirit artistry." If someone wants it, during a session I draw a picture of a person close to them who has died. I do not see a photo first and often times I am told nothing about the person I am drawing. But this drawing provides additional proof that the person I'm reading really is coming through and is "alive."

How do people feel about these somewhat eerie pictures you draw? Very positive. It proves the continuity of life, and gives those in the spirit world a voice and a face. It gives them peace of mind that their loved ones are still alive and well and watching over them in the spirit world.

What did Bob Olsen, who is probably the best known personality in the metaphysical field, say of you: [Reading] "One of these incredibly gifted, although not so famous, psychic mediums ...she may not be widely known across the country, she has already earned a high reputation among Bostonians, even many New Englanders. ... And being a counselor, Rita is professionally capable of dealing with the many issues that may come up during a reading, bereavement issues being just one....

"But it is Rita's spirit artistry that clearly sets her gift apart from other psychic mediums, and allows her to give something extra to her clients. But she doesn't need her drawings to alter one's life with her readings. Her gift of spirit communication alone can change the course of one's life."

The provocative titles of two of your books are "Do Dead People See You Shower?" and "Do Dead People Walk Their Dogs?" What is the answer? Yes! They see us in the bathroom and they see us in the bedroom and everywhere! But who cares? They're dead! Who are they gonna tell anything? You never think about God looking. It's the same thing.

What will it be like for us when we're dead? People who have been there tell me the next life is so much better than this one. This is the classroom and that's home.
Everything is beautiful. There are no problems, no mortgage payments. We'll have fun and may even want to shock or kid people who are still here. In fact, I've twice had a spirit actually try to make love to me. I had one client whose beach house had a very playful resident ghost. He seemed to live in their shower and delighted in pressing up against anyone who used it!

What will we look like? We'll be asexual and we won't wear clothes because shadows don't like to be burdened by Prada or Louis Vuitton purses. Anyone can tell that I'm not dead yet! Bring on the bling! Gimme the bangles, baubles and beads — and then help me hide the credit card bills from my husband.

Will all of us go to this beautiful place? Evil people don't go to the same place you and I will. They'll be someplace else, paying for their past sins. Like O.J. He loves to play golf and there's no golf on the other side.

Do people who were evil in this life have the opportunity to change? When a criminal reaches the other side and works through how hurtful he's been to people he's destroyed, he will try to come through with blessings. Take someone like Bernie Madoff. He will try to repay his victims from the other side, if those he stole from are still here when he gets there! But it goes both ways. His victims have to open themselves up, because if they set up a wall of negativity, the blessings will not be able to reach them.

If we're not a professional medium like you, can we call up someone on the other side? Yes, but be prepared. Say that you want to see some sign of someone who has passed on, like your mother. They will show it to you. Maybe not then because I always tell people: "You can't call them up on a dime." But communication is possible if you want to. And if you want them to leave, you can simply tell them to go and they will.

Are you ever frightened of those on the other side? As I told *The New York Times* "Dead people don't scare me but living people occasionally do." Seriously, dead people are not judging us, so we don't have to be scared of or worry what they're thinking. It's not like they're going, "Whoa! Has she got a big butt!" or "If I was him, I'da shaved that!" or "Holy Moly! Did ya ever see such a big ..." Well, you get the point.

What was life like for you before you became professional? When I was young I wanted to talk to guys, not talk to dead guys. School was hard for me because I was very dyslexic. Plus, I'm deaf in my left ear, since I was born with no opening there.

When I got older, I became a receptionist, which in a way I still am. I'm still receiving messages and passing them on, just from different people in a different way.

How would you describe yourself? Basically, I'm just your average Jersey girl who talks to the dead. I consider myself to be a spiritual person. But I'm hardly perfect. I can swear like a sailor, I enjoy a good dirty joke, and I don't get along with my pickle-puss mother-in-law. She's been a real rock in my underwear.

What do you think of people who are skeptical of your abilities? I think of it like television shows. If you don't like a program, don't watch it. People want too much. Some aren't happy unless they get the combination to the safe!

What's the difference between a medium and a psychic? A medium is a psychic, but a psychic is not necessarily a medium. Someone who is just psychic can give you a prediction, but they can't tell you where or who they got it from. I can tell you who on the other side is bringing the message.

Everyone says they've read for royalty but you really have. Can you give names? No. But *The New York Times* said that my "fan base...includes Sarah Ferguson (member of Britain's royalty), the actresses Edie Falco and Julia Louis-Dreyfus and readers in 10 languages...The dead have been my best publicists," they quoted me as saying. I have also been quoted as having read for the cast of *The Sopranos* and the Baldwin brothers.

When did you first realize you had this gift? The first actual "human" form I first saw was Saint Francis of Assisi standing on our lawn when I was a child. I didn't know who he was until I was older. I also saw geometric shapes floating through the air that I now believe were waves of energy.

What other careers or jobs have you had? I was an accountant and comptroller. I am a certified breath therapist, Yoga teacher, certified birth and labor doula, childbirth educator and lactation educator.

How does accounting differ from psychic work? In my career, I went from preparing financial statements to providing services as an intuitive/psychic. This was a leap from pure 'left brain' work to extreme 'right brain' intuition. As I grew more confident with my "sight," and as I added other healing modalities to my "bag of tricks," it just sort of took on a life of its own that doing intuitive readings was the most direct and healing service I could offer, and that I could supplement it with what I had learned in other careers. But while I was as in the financial field earlier, I kept my intuitive abilities quiet because my clients were hiring me for other reasons.

Were there any challenges being a doula? I attended more than 150 births, offering emotional, informational and physical support to pregnant women prenatally, during labor and post-partum. The longest job I had lasted 33 hours straight and involved the birth of two children to two different sets of parents, one right after the other. After the first birth, I was exhausted and closed my eyes for 45 minutes. Then I wound up staying with the second client for 14 hours.

Do you advise parents as well as assisting in the birth? Ob/gyns often lack the time to sit with their patients and answer all their questions and the patients are often embarrassed to ask. As a lactation educator, I was able to answer questions, often practical as well as emotional support to new moms with breastfeeding—anything from the proper positioning of the baby while nursing, latch-on techniques, and when to burp the baby!

What do you do for the mothers during labor? As a doula presiding at births, my sight was helpful as I was able to see blocked energy in the delivery room—such as the position of the bed, an attitude or another family member whose energy or presence was making my client uncomfortable. Once we kindly suggested that that family member get a cup of tea, my client's labor resumed and progressed in a regular pattern; the distressing "block" had been removed. I could also help them breathe through certain tough times and even know what to pack in their hospital bag because I could "see" what lay ahead for them.

You say that you can tell by phone if someone is pregnant? I was on a phone reading with a client who was calling to primarily ask about work, transitions in moving and her husband's company. Within the first five minutes I asked if she was pregnant? She quickly said she was not. I said, "I see that you are pregnant and you're going to have a baby girl." She took a pregnancy test and phoned back a couple of hours later to tell me she was in fact, pregnant! And five months later she contacted me to say that they were expecting a girl.

How did you get started professionally? After working as an accountant for several years, I suffered from carpal tunnel and a number of other physical disturbances, no doubt from sitting at a computer and cranking numbers all day. I didn't like the work and apparently nor did my body. I ventured into many other healing modalities in an attempt to heal myself. At first, I was very reluctant to become a professional psychic because I had no idea how I could make a living doing something as unconventional as giving intuitive readings after being an accountant!

Why did you become a certified breath therapist? While recovering from bi-lateral carpal tunnel syndrome, I began receiving guided breathing sessions to help heal my wrists. The session not only helped to minimize pain and discomfort but also provided a deep mental stillness. I went on to become certified in 'breatherapy' and began offering this service to both individual clients and groups.

Why are some clients more difficult to work with? Clients who are very angry, cynical or closed can often change the flow and positivity of a session. For some, seeing a psychic might bring up nervous reactions and fears. These people sit down with their arms crossed over their chest and say, "Okay Nicki, tell me what you see." This shields them from receiving the true healing nature of our time together. We co-create the field of healing together. If someone is closed or unwilling to "do the dance" together, it makes my job more difficult.

PSYCHIC

MARY T. BROWNE

(212) 242-6080

www.MaryTBrowne.com

This internationally famous New York and Connecticut psychic, teacher and author was described in Forbes as "Wall Street's psychic advisor," but she has clients in all walks of life.

BOOKS: "Love in Action," "Life after Death," "The Power of Karma," "The 5 Rules of Thought: How to Use the Power of Your Mind to Get What You Want."

To schedule a phone or in-person reading, call (212) 242-6080

How did you become the best known psychic in America today? I have had more than 8,000 clients over 25 years. I've been on *Larry King Live*, *Weekend Today*, *CNN*, *Fox and Friends*, *Good Morning America Now*, *Good Day New York* and featured in *Forbes*, *Marie Claire*, *New York*, *Worth*, *American Health*, *Elle*, *Vogue*, *The New York Times* and many other newspapers and magazines. I've been a guest on over 400 radio shows, and the psychic character in the movie *Light Sleeper* was based on me.

Why do you only do three to four readings a day when with your popularity, you could be doing a dozen? People have no idea that it takes an enormous amount of concentration, energy and focus in order to give an individual reading. It might look easy, but it is exhausting. I want to give each client the best possible session, so I limit the number of people I see.

How did you know you were psychic? I was born with a psychic gift. When I was seven years old I was at my aunt's funeral parlor in Iowa. I had been asked to answer the phones while she ran errands. I saw the spirit of a woman standing in front of a coffin arranging flowers. When I walked up to the coffin and looked in I realized the dead woman was the spirit that I had seen. I told my grandmother what had happened and she said, "You have a gift, don't scare people and don't brag about it."

Do you do any mediumistic work? Yes. Messages do come to me from the spirit world. But most of my work concerns this world and not the next one. I cannot promise clients that they will receive a communication from a departed loved one. I believe the spirits choose to communicate with us and that we cannot force them to do that. In my book "Life after Death" I speak about my visions of the spirit world and share stories of people who have received messages from the departed through me.
Too often people interchange the words "psychic" and "medium." A medium is a channel or a conduit. All mediums are not psychics. I am both a psychic and a medium.

Do you feel that you're a therapist? No. A person tells a therapist: "This is what happened to me." The psychic tells the person. "This is what I see happening to you." The therapist helps the person figure out what's wrong. The psychic tells them what is wrong. I have been called a psychic life coach because I help my clients get their lives into greater harmony whether it's personal or financial.

What do you do for your clients? I can look at their lives, see what the future holds, and help them take the steps to achieve their goals with the least amount of trouble. I'm not trying to sell anyone a fantasy. There are ways of learning how to think that will make a person much happier. As I said in my book "The 5 Rules of Thought," people should decide what they want, see it happen, stick to the plan, believe it can work, and work at the problem until they get the results they want.

What are people most concerned with? It used to be love, love, love. Now it's money, money, money. People are frightened. They want to know if they will keep their current job. Or if they have none, when they will get a job again. You can't think about love when you can't pay the rent.

Are some people harder for you to read than others? Certain people appear to be easier to read because they have a lot more going on in their lives than others. I may see in one client's future that they are falling in love and moving to Italy to open a restaurant. But in another client, that they are going to remain living in their apartment, going to the same job and being with their current partner. There may be the perception that the person with more going on is easier to read, but that has not been my experience.

Any advice for people who are worried about the future? Almost everybody is worried about the future. Millions have lost their homes, their jobs or both. People must find ways to deal with what is and not with what was. This is a time to focus on community, family, adaptability and on the spiritual side of life. The only way to overcome worry is through action. Countless people have started their own business because they lost their jobs. This is a time when people need to focus on their inner strength.

There is a Divine Force waiting to help us. When we direct our thoughts towards the Divine Force we begin to think and act in greater harmony. This makes difficult things seem easier and promotes a feeling of happiness and replaces thoughts of worry and failure with thoughts of action and success.

PSYCHIC

LITANY BURNS

www.LitanyBurns.com
www.intuitivenation.com

Litany Burns is a cutting edge medium and clairvoyant, who has read for European royalty and celebrities like Madonna and helped identify the Son of Sam

BOOKS: "Develop Your Psychic Abilities," "The Sixth Sense of Children."
VIDEOS: "Develop Your Psychic Powers," "Children Among Us."

To schedule a phone, Skype or in-person reading,
e-mail litany@litanyburns.com

Do you enjoy being psychic? Sometimes it can be frustrating. If you tell somebody that you're a writer, no one asks you to write something on the spot. But if you tell someone you're a psychic, they immediately ask you some question or try to make you prove yourself to them in some way.

Why do you think people should go to psychics? Psychics can help people get more in touch with their own abilities. They can also help them choose more wisely in personal relationships and help them with other decisions, whether it's selecting a date, a plumber, a babysitter, or a stock. Psychics can help people cut to the chase. They can help someone be less likely to get caught up in a relationship that's bad or buy a lemon.

Do clients generally take your advice? I'll give you an example of someone who didn't. A French producer came to see me about a side business venture. He wanted to open an exclusive restaurant with several partners. He gave me letters to hold with the signatures of his potential partners.
I told him in great detail the problems he would personally have with each of his partners in this venture. He also gave me the name of the restaurant written on a piece of paper, and I held it and told him I felt he should not invest in it. I later heard he invested three hundred fifty thousand dollars and the restaurant never opened. He lost all of his money.

What did you see in the Son of Sam case? The Son of Sam was a madman who terrorized the outer boroughs of New York City by shooting beautiful women, most of them long-haired brunettes. They were generally in deserted places, sometimes with their boyfriends, often in a car.
Near the end of the killings, I was called in by the D.A.'s office. I used psychometry and held onto a private letter written to journalist Jimmy Breslin from someone who called himself Son of Sam.
I was able to tell that the killer was adopted, that one of his biological parents had died, that he worked in a post office in the Bronx, that there would be another killing, and that there would be an eyewitness. Also that soon after that final killing, he would be apprehended for something that had nothing to do with the case. These predictions came true, and David Berkowitz was picked up because of a parking ticket he got in an area near the last shooting.

What was the most unusual situation in which you were asked for advice?
When I first started reading, a woman I knew nothing about told me she was involved in a lawsuit. She wanted to know if she was going to win because all

her money was tied up in it.

I saw this small man with a mustache and bald head in a desert area, and I told her that something bad was going to happen to him. I told her that she would get some of her money back, and the man was going to be exposed. On her way out, I asked her, "By the way, who are you suing?" She said, "I'm suing the Shah of Iran!" Of course, a few years later, he was exposed and ousted. I assume she got some of her money back.

Do you remember the first time you were fascinated by something psychic? When I was twelve, a country kid from upstate New York, my family and I went to New York City and visited a big toy store. I was told I could buy only one toy. I was drawn to a Ouija board, although I had no idea what it was. I kept going back to it and looking at it, trying to figure out what it was. I wound up buying it. At home with the Ouija board, I immediately started talking to a spirit. I've been talking to him ever since. He is my oldest and nearest friend, and we have helped a lot of people together.

Whom do you read for now? I've read for everyone right up to royalty, an Italian prince and a duchess, and even Madonna, who I read for twice in the early 90's.

Do you also do healing? Yes, like the time a seventy year-old woman client was having open-heart surgery. Her daughter called me at her mother's request and asked me if I would send her healing energy at a specific time on the day when she was having the operation 150 miles away.

I did and soon heard her mother's voice in my head. She told me she had left her body and was happily visiting with her deceased husband. I urged her to return to her body on the operating table immediately.

When I later spoke with her daughter and told her what I saw, she was speechless. Her mother's heart had stopped beating at exactly the time I was communicating with her, and the doctors were about to pronounce her dead when her heart began beating on its own. She survived the operation and lived for many more years.

PSYCHIC

DOLORES CARDELUCCI

DoloresAgeless@gmail.com

www.AgelessMind.com

A senior psychic at 83 and best known for her real estate tips, she has also read for such A-listers as George Clooney, Brad Pitt, Kelsey Grammer, Paula Abdul, Courteney Cox and Jennifer Anniston.

Books: "Trust in Today," "The Setup."

Do you think you're the oldest successful psychic today? Experience matters; age doesn't. That's why my web site and e-mail is "Ageless Mind."

Are most of your clients men or women? I'm really mostly a business reader. Therefore, a lot of my clients are men. I do career stuff. I'm very good with numbers because I once worked as an auditor and bookkeeper. I don't see the psychic junkies. I'm not a Band-Aid.

Do you have any business specialties? Yes, I'm good for seeing ahead regarding real estate, and a lot of people come to me for tips. Not just where people will move to, or which house is best for them, but since I have so many big business clients, where their company should move to, or what property is best for them to buy. *LA Weekly* called me "the best psychic portal into the murky future."

Who are some of the A-list celebrities you've read for? Paula Abdul, Brad Pitt, Kelsey Grammer—I've written pilots for him—Courteney Cox, Jennifer Aniston and others. George Clooney used my talents for citing people and places to avoid. Some say I told him about the villa in Italy he would buy. I told Sharon Stone she would get the part in *Casino. In Style* magazine described how when Paula Abdul and Brad Beckerman met and fell in love in February of 1996, he confessed on the second date that he had gone to me and I had told her that would marry someone named Julie (Paula Abdul is really Paula Julie), fall in love in February and I saw the word "Florida," which is where he went to school.

You've had a colorful life. Tell us about it. I was born to a devout Italian Catholic family in South Philly. Besides seeing to God's business, they also saw to the Mob's business, if you know what I mean. I started giving readings to people, but didn't think of it as a vocation but more of an avocation. Meanwhile, I worked for the renowned fashion and film designer William Travilla as his personal assistant, and also did his auditing and bookkeeping. Our last film together was *Valley of the Dolls*. I also invested in and owned several chiropractic clinics, but found them boring. So I opened a clothing store and then a restaurant called Cardelucci's Italian Restaurant in Westwood. But all during this I continued to read clients.

Do you advise on health matters? Yes I do and I am very good at it. And since I'm a cancer survivor—I've had two recent bouts with it and successful surgery—I tell the world, and women in particular, that cancer can be conquered. There is life after a diagnosis of any life-altering threat.

Do you spend most of your time giving readings? No, I've written books. And for the last 20 years have taught *The Course In Miracles* and have facilitated a couple of workshops each year. In these workshops I teach the true nature of forgiveness and a spiritual way to accomplish each person's dreams and goals. I volunteer my time for the Course and the workshops. The participants' donations go directly to the Church.

Do you do traditional psychic work? I do some numerology. I'm also a psychometry reader. I tune in by holding onto something you own, like a watch or a piece of jewelry, handwriting sample or business card. If people want to talk about their love life, I tell them to bring a significant person's photo.

Do you consider yourself to be "spiritual"? I think the word is overused and overrated. I don't like the images of turbans and crystal balls, or in movies, ghostly moans and rattling chains. I believe we're all psychics. We all have intuitive sense, but people don't act on it because they don't believe they have it.

When did you realize you were intuitive? As a teenager I became aware of a deep intuitive inner voice that gave me a heightened understanding of other people's lives, hopes, fears and aspirations. Without formally giving it a name, I began giving "readings" to my close friends. Soon strangers who had heard of my gift were seeking me out for counsel and guidance.

How would you describe yourself? I'm complicated. I am an intuitive spiritualist and devout church lady, I attended Catholic school and spent many hours a day with the nuns in the convent, which was the beginning of my religious and spiritual journey—which has never ended. On the other hand, I can be as tough and coarse as a South Philly truck driver—which has saved me many times.

What is your philosophy of life? Life is a banquet and everyone is entitled to feast on God's abundance both here on Earth and beyond.

41

ASTROLOGER

ARLENE DAHL

Dahlmark Productions, PO Box 116
Sparkill, New York 10976

*As psychic as she is beautiful, she has starred in thirty movies
and nineteen plays and authored thirteen books on
astrology and beauty.*

For more information, contact: Dahlmark Productions, PO Box 116
Sparkill, New York 10976

What were your most dramatic psychic experiences? I had three out-of-body experiences. The first time, I was in a terrible automobile accident. The convertible I was in turned over twice—and we didn't have seat belts then. I was unconscious, doctors couldn't find a pulse, and I didn't appear to be breathing. The doctors were examining me on the table in the emergency ward, and I saw and felt myself floating below the ceiling, looking down at myself on the table and at what they were doing. When I came to—and back into my body—I was in intensive care. I remembered what had happened, and told the doctor where he had been standing, how everyone had been positioned around me, and the conversations that went on.

What about the other times? The second time was a horseback riding accident, and the third time was during my son Lorenzo's birth, in which we both almost lost our lives.

When did you get into tea leaf reading? After my long recovery period from the auto accident, I was invited to a weekend party and had found a book called "Tea Leaf Reading at a Glance." To amuse the guests, I brought along some gold earrings, an off-the-shoulder blouse, and a colorful Gypsy skirt. I came out in my Gypsy outfit, lit some candles, and started reading the symbols. I put the book aside and read what I saw of my own interpretations. The more I trusted my own intuition, the more on target I was.

Do you remember any of your successful readings that night? I told one gentleman, who I later discovered was the head of CBS, that he would have a success the following spring with a little girl who had the initial E next to her curly head. He was shocked, because the television series *Eloise* had just been signed for production that morning. He confessed, "No one here knows about that, not even my wife!"

Did you continue your forecasts? No, I decided to drop it because I became frightened at my own accuracy! Six months later, however, I was making a film in London where they served tea twice a day. I started reading tea leaves again, and went back to it because I realized that through this medium, I could help people. Carroll Righter, the dean of American astrologers, later became my guru. Every star in those days had readings with him, including Marlene Dietrich, Ronald Reagan, and Jane Wyman.

What were these books about? In 1950 I was the first to combine astrology with beauty and fashion in my syndicated beauty column. Simon & Schuster then asked me to write twelve astrology books about beauty, one for each sign of the zodiac, and my "Beautyscope" books sold over three million each. Then I wrote a book on astrological relationships, called "Lovescopes," which became a popular cable television series.

Do you always tell people what you see? I was taught by Carroll Righter not to be an alarmist. If someone asked me about a trip they were about to take and I felt that the plane may have engine trouble, I would try to persuade them to put off the flight, explaining it would be better timed and more successful if they went later.

Do you use your intuitive gifts with your husband? Yes, in fact, when I met my husband, Marc Rosen, at a business meeting, I went up to him and said, "Hello, Libra." He was stunned. I said, "I'll bet you were born around the end of September, around the twenty-ninth or thirtieth." He turned white and said, "Yes, the thirtieth." We became instant friends. He is a famous package designer and recently won his fourth Fifi designer award for Halston's men's fragrance.

Did you make predictions for your former husband, Fernando Lamas? Often. He was always rather skeptical until I told him that a musical he was up for with Ethel Merman in New York would bring him much success and Broadway accolades. Of course it did.

How have your forecasts helped your son, Lorenzo Lamas? He wanted a part in a new TV series written by Stephen Cannell. When he didn't get it, he called me, and I told him to go out and celebrate because something even better would come to him the following week. Ten days later he was offered the lead in the new series *Renegade*, produced by Stephen Cannell.

Did you use your psychic abilities when you were making movies? Yes, for example, I read Blake Edwards's tea leaves and told him, "You're going to make a comedy next year, and the star's initials are ES." Blake said, "You're right. I'm directing *A Shot in the Dark* next spring. You've got the S right for Sophia, but it should be L for Loren. She's agreed to star in it." But Sophia Loren dropped out of the film and was replaced by Elke Sommer!

How did your compassion for animals develop? I grew up on a farm in England where there were no other children to play with. I also had a serious hearing loss that made it difficult for me to communicate with people. But animals communicate telepathically, using mental images and physical feelings that don't depend on hearing. So the animals became my best friends.

What is an early memory of yours about animals that's not a happy one? Three of my best friends were geese, given to me by my father to raise. When they were nine months old, my father killed them for our Christmas dinner. I was horrified, realizing that other people did not have the same gift with animals and feelings about them as I did.

How do you comfort people whose pets have passed on? When an animal passes over, their pain is over, while the pain of our grief is only beginning. But people should realize that animals live on in spirit, just as people do. As I say in my book with the same title, there are no sad dogs—cats, turtles, horses, birds, cows—in heaven.

How do you know our pets are in the spirit world? I get a mental image of them, just as if I asked you about the Statue of Liberty and you would immediately see it in your eyes.

How can you help a dying pet? Some animals need permission to leave their earthly bodies if they think their owners aren't ready to let them go. I put my hands on them and ask God and my spirit guides to let them know that if they need to pass over into the spirit realm, it's OK.

Can someone contact a pet they once had? Yes, because they're still here. He or she has been with you in both animal and human form in many past lives. In fact, you have been a dog in a past life and have been with him before. If you are enlightened, so are the animals that come into your lives.

Do pets also grieve when one of them passes on? When you have more than one pet and one dies, they're often devastated—and confused. They feel the presence of the missing one around but can't see the physical body. They don't realize that the missing one "has gone home" and that the animal is still with them.

Do they ever contact us after they die? As I said in "There Are No Sad

Dogs In Heaven," they are constantly sending out that energy of love, like radio waves, into the electromagnetic field of the universe, because there is no separation between one planet and the other.

They remain with us, and may come to us, sometimes even sleeping with us in their usual place on the bed. If we let them know that we miss them, they will give us a sign that they're there—sometimes visiting us in our dreams. We just have to be open and receptive to their presence.

What about people who can't let go of a deceased dog or cat? One of my clients kept her dog's ashes in a container by her bed when she slept—and another kept his cat's body in the freezer! Some continue to put out food and water afterwards. I tell them that while their pet remains connected to us, they no longer need earthly things, like their bodies or ashes or food to remain connected to our world.

Do you get any calls that surprise you? I hear from a lot of long-distance truck drivers, who listen to my phone in show and are on the road for long periods of time. They often travel with their dogs.

What did you do before you became a famous animal communicator? I lived in London for a while, pursuing a fashion and modeling career in all the major fashion capitals in Europe. But, I had a spiritual experience in 1994 that led me to start practicing my gift.

How many pets do you have? I live in Texas where there's enough wide open spaces that I have nine cats, four dogs, one horse, and three frogs.

Can I see or hear you now on TV or radio? Many segments of "The Pet Psychic," my hit TV series on *Animal Planet* are now on YouTube [See "Sonya Fitzpatrick."] I have a popular call-in radio show on Sirius-XM, *Animal Intuition*, on Sundays from 5pm-7pm Eastern Time. I use my telepathic gifts and healing talents to counsel thousands of callers. I also have another website, www.alettertomydog.com And yes, I do private readings.

DOUGALL FRASER

customerservice@DougallFraser.com
(877) 936-8425
www.DougallFraser.com

This author, psychic & cosmic coach, calls himself "The Queer Guy with the Third Eye," and he was named Best Psychic in Dallas, and one of the country's top clairvoyants by Spin magazine and The New York Post.

www.facebook.com/theofficialdougallfraserfanpage
www.twitter.com/dougallfraser

BOOKS: "But You Knew That Already: What a Psychic Can Teach You About Life."

To schedule a phone or in-person reading, call
(877) 936-8425

Why do you call one chapter in your book "But You Knew that Already," "Mini-Merlin?" I was obsessed with the occult at that age. I purchased my first deck of tarot cards around the age of eight and started giving readings. While other kids were playing cops and robbers, I would light a candle and hold a penny, trying to contact Abe Lincoln. I was a unique child.

What did you study in school? I was never pulled by traditional education, probably due to my control issues. Like a true Taurus, I would study the opposite of anything my teachers assigned. I was a bit stubborn at that age. My math teacher told me "If you spent as much time studying geometry as tarot cards, you'd do really well." But what was I going to do with geometry? I dropped out of high school during my junior year, due to a messy divorce that my parents were going through. Things were stressful at home, so I moved to Texas to be closer to my sister. And let's be honest, Texas seems like the perfect place for a closeted psychic to move to, right?

What did the Dallas Observer say about you? "Topping out at 6 feet 6 inches...one 45-minute reading is likely to regurgitate five years' worth of therapy over the tarot deck... if this guy isn't truly clairvoyant, he's intuitive as hell and... what's the difference?" To this day, I had the largest response from that article that I ever have. And I've been on the *Dr. Phil* show!

You had some funny descriptions in your book about your brief attempts to work at psychic fairs and at psychic hot lines. Working a psychic fair is like being a short order cook. People want answers now. They race from psychic to psychic. You might read for 24 people, back to back, all day. It's a fascinating experience and a great way for a psychic to learn how to tune in to their client quickly. It certainly prepared me for my late night adventures on the psychic hot lines.

What type of callers called you on the psychic hot lines? As a teenager, I would stay up late at night to watch psychic hotline infomercials. Dionne Warwick, host of the Psychic Friends Network infomercial, started to feel like a distant cousin. It seemed like the perfect job opportunity for someone in my position.

Unfortunately, once I started, I became very disillusioned with their practices. The callers were mostly on welfare, so a $5 a minute call didn't seem like the best life choice for them. I was getting calls from people who were beaten by their spouses, and many callers wanted to know when their sons would get out of prison. People were in pain and in dire need of answers, but this business model was not the right fit for me. In my opinion, those networks were interested in making money above all else.

You were a co-host on a TV show called That Sex Show. What did you discuss? *That Sex Show* was a live, call-in advice show focused on sex, love, and relationships. It was an exciting platform, and a dramatic shift to go from giving advice about chakras to giving advice on oral sex. As the psychic on the panel, my job was to tune in to the emotional and spiritual needs of our callers.

Why do you feel color is so important? I believe that color is the language of the universe. When I tune in to someone, I initially see color and energy around them. Those colors tell me about their strengths and weaknesses, their hopes and desires. I can teach people to use color to create and change their lives for the better.

What is Cosmic Coaching? Cosmic Coaching is a service that I created to help my clients achieve their goals. My version of life coaching combines psychology, meditation, practical advice, color therapy, and other modalities. During a Cosmic Coaching package, we set goals and homework assignments that hold you accountable towards living your best life.

How do you get people to open up about something they'd rather not discuss? I find that the best way to help a client open up about something is for me to be vulnerable first. Often times I will share a personal story of a painful experience that I had to confront or move through, that is similar to a storyline I see in their life. For example, if I see sexual abuse in a client's past, I will share my own experience as an abuse survivor as well. This makes the environment safe for them to open up, and the healing process can begin.

Do you do medium work? I can talk to the dead but I prefer to talk to the living. Once I contact Aunt Tutty, after we establish that she died from pancreatic cancer and had a cat named Isabella, where does that leave us? I'm more interested in finding out what makes people tick and helping them change their current lives.

Tell us about your Amish-Mennonite background. Amish-Mennonites are similar to the Amish in beliefs and clothes. They are also strongly communal, and every parent is a parent to others in the community. They emphasize the Bible, and my family regularly gathered in a circle for Bible readings. My father's voice was hypnotic, and I often drifted away with spirit entities that were teaching me.

My father also developed the first yellow geranium. He could have had it patented, but the Amish-Mennonites do not believe in receiving recognition and money for the creation of nature.

What is your first memory of doing a healing? In the 3rd grade, I received a vision of my mother falling. Without permission from the teacher I dashed out of the school and ran over a mile, all the way home where I found my mother lying on the floor. She was very sick and vomiting. I placed my small hands on her body and prayed to the angels to heal her. She improved immediately and when I looked down at my hands, they were black, as if I had extracted a poison from her body.

Did you stay in the healing professions before you became a professional intuitive? I became a nurse, then an X-ray technician, and later a chairside dental assistant. The dentist that I worked for was always amazed that I knew which instruments to hand to him before he asked for them! Those jobs were not for me, but they did help me gain a greater understanding of death, dying and anatomy.

Describe your near death experience after an early suicide attempt. I had left home at age 14 because I wanted to continue my education. Amish-Mennonite children finish school after the eighth grade. I did not speak much because I had a stuttering problem (which I later overcame with two years of singing lessons), and I felt lonely and alone. Finally, my depression became so great that I took pills. While I was unconscious, I became aware of floating up toward the ceiling and looking down at my body. I could see many spirit doctors and nurses working to revive me. Their faces were glowing with love and I could hear heavenly music.

A Spirit Guide named Rose came to me and told me: "If you will follow me, I will lead you to a new life." I knew I was being given a choice. I could continue toward the magnificent light or return to my body. As wonderful as it was outside of my body, I said to myself: "I have to return and tell everyone about the Spiritual world."

Tell us about Lily Dale. Lily Dale is one of the largest Spiritualist communities of the Modern Spiritualist movement. It's located in Chautauqua County, NY, approximately one hour south of Buffalo, NY. There are approximately 275 residents. Every summer Lily Dale opens its gates and over 40,000 visitors come for workshops, lectures, church services and mediumship readings.

Describe your JFK assassination prediction. I saw in 1960 that Senator Kennedy was going to win the election—and also that he would be assassinated. Every time I saw him on TV I became surer of my prediction. Late in 1962 I became so convinced of his imminent death that I even called the White House to warn him—three times!—but they wouldn't put me through.

Could you have changed the course of history if you had told him not to go to Dallas? Psychics can foresee future events which hold the potential to change the course of history. But it is useless if no one will listen to them. But there is a difference between a prediction and a prophecy. A prediction can be changed, but a prophecy is already set. Even if I'd been able to get through to President Kennedy, and he cancelled his trip, he might have met the same end at a different time and different place. But it might have happened at the very end of his presidency, giving him more time to accomplish his goals.

What are your beliefs about death and the afterlife? The fact that we can communicate with loved ones in spirit proves the continuity of life and that there is no death. The spirit simply leaves the physical form and gravitates to another level of consciousness and awareness. Through the medium's connection with spirit, our departed loved ones continue to connect with us still here on the earth plane.

Do you see spirits all the time? No, it's like being a radio, where you tune in to different stations. I can sit in a room and everything is tuned out. But I can tune into a certain frequency and communicate with those on the other side.

Do spirits sometimes happen when you're not tuned in? Yes, they can appear spontaneously. That often happens because they have an urgent message to deliver.

PSYCHIC (SPECIALTY: LOVE)

CHRISTOPHER GOLDEN

psychic@outlook.com

www.psychic90210.com

The Wall Street Journal called him the Beverly Hills "Psychic to the Stars" but he is best known as a love psychic.

www.facebook.com/pages/Beverly-Hills-Psychic-Christopher-
Golden/358186677619834
www.Twitter.com/90210Psychic

To schedule a phone reading, go to
www.psychic90210.com/bookonlinenow.html

How did you go from being famous as a Beverly Hills celebrity psychic to a love advisor? Everyone asks about love: stopping a divorce, reuniting with a lover, ending cheating. Most of my clients don't want to leave something that important to chance, regardless of their status in society. So they seek reliable psychic advice. If you don't believe you deserve the best, you will never have it.

Can you help these people? I can help someone who wants to be helped. Usually the initial question is never about what it appears to be. It's really a jumping off point. People who come to me generally don't want a traditional psychic reading. They're interested in changing future outcomes. That is my focus.

Do people ask you to perform "love spells"? Love spells don't work and to do so would violate my own religious convictions. They are based on superstition and most of the people advertising them are scam artists and phonies who are going to lie to you. I tell people the truth. I don't use Black Magic, spells, unicorns, rainbows, dream catchers or crystal balls. If I can help you reunite using genuine metaphysics, I will put my heart and soul into it.

What are the people who call you really looking for? Often someone is looking for a quick fix to a surface problem, but I feel the soul is reaching out. I try to help them move beyond their question and deepen their spiritual journey. People who come to me are essentially asking, "Who am I?" My role is to help people become the best version of themselves they can be—and to enable them to have fulfilling loving relationships which give their life depth and meaning.

Why would people go to a psychic rather than a therapist? Psychology deals with human behavior, which doctors either try to talk or drug people into changing. An authentic psychic deals with the whole person—mind, body and spirit. Reputable psychics are less focused on telling you trivial information, such as when you will be traveling, for example, than on working on a transformation to create a greater sense of possibility for their clients. Would you rather spend years talking about how your father didn't go to enough of your Little League games or would you prefer to talk to someone with a mastery of metaphysics, who can see around corners and show you how to get what you want?

How accurate are you? There are a lot of psychic websites that advertise that they're 100 percent accurate. How are they measuring this? Who can say? People give me feedback, and it seems I am mostly pretty much on, but I don't think anyone is perfectly accurate all the time. I am not 100 percent accurate. No one is.

How did you get started professionally? I was raised in Beverly Hills, and word of mouth spread there. When people heard that I was accurate, that led to being asked to give psychic readings in people's trailers on film sets and television productions, etc. Ironically, many people try to "break into" being a psychic to the show biz crowd, but the role really came looking for me.

Why is it important for a celebrity to go to a psychic like you for advice? I will never confirm the names of any clients I have worked with. That said, celebrities are a commodity, a brand. They support a lot of people—and many of those people are a part of their support system. So their decisions have a big impact.

For example, a famous athlete who gets into trouble may put a lot of people all over the world out of business if he can no longer endorse a brand. So the brand has to be protected (sometimes from itself) and it's often an agent or manager who comes to me first. A Hollywood psychic with a proven track record just makes good business sense.

Are most of your clients rich and famous? More than 95 percent of my clients are neither rich nor famous, and people shouldn't come to me because of that anyway. If you have a pipe burst in your home, do you want a "plumber to the stars" or do you want the best plumber?

I don't use my client roster as a calling card. I have read for everyone from royalty to bus drivers. I charge an affordable amount for a 15-minute psychic reading, so that everyday people can take charge of their future as well, not just the elite.

I don't perform at parties or fairs. They're side show attractions for people's amusement. That's what magicians and balloon animals are for. I prefer to work by phone or online, but mostly, I just prefer to make a difference in people's lives. That is the purpose of having such a gift as this.

Do you own horses? Yes. I live in Stillwater, Oklahoma, with my husband, Lenn. We raise registered quarter horses, Lenn trains futurity barrel horses and team roping horses. With everything that happens training horses, my gift to read and heal horses and other animals is put to use every day.

Do you know when a horse will not make it? Not always. Toward the end, it may show in their energy field. I remember the story of Edgar Cayce and the elevator. He had been in a department store, looking at red sweaters. When the elevator doors opened, he realized the people inside had no color around them, their energy was gone. So he didn't get on the elevator, which crashed to the basement, killing all aboard. When your time is up, the energy leaves naturally.

Give an example of a horse who has lost its energy. I was doing a metaphysical reading on a very nice mare. I used the information on her registration papers which identified her, and I had trouble picking up her energy. I couldn't understand why.
I went to see her, and she looked fine. I did another reading several hours later, and could not get any energy at all. I went out to check on her and she had just died. That was shocking to me, and happens rarely as energy always is, it just changes form.

How did you get interested in horses? I was brought up on a ranch in Idaho, which brought me eye to eye with Mother Nature. We had baby colts and puppies. My sister and I spoiled the puppies rotten, dressing them up in doll clothes and such.

Describe your healing ability with horses. I had no idea that I had this gift until I started using the information from a class I had taken. I developed my gift by using it and having results. Horses that were sore and hurt: after working on them their pain was gone, whether it be hands on healing or metaphysical. Word of mouth is the best advertisement. People started calling for help, my clientele grew and miracles happened. Now 30 years later, wonderful, and miraculous things continue to happen and for this I give great thanks and gratitude.

Specifically, how did you heal them? I hold my hands over their bodies and feel blocked energy, I then lay my hand on them allowing energy to flow through me until the blocked energy is cleared and soreness is gone. Sometimes horses will almost go to sleep, their breathing will change and they get very relaxed.

What happened the first time you tried it? I was riding a nice gelding, and he started limping. I got off and ran my hands down his leg, where energy was blocked; I held my hands on the area until it read clear. I led him and he walked off sound, I was shocked and thought it was a coincidence.

Did you automatically know what to do? Yes, I was listening to myself, just surprised it worked. Animals are great teachers of unconditional love we don't always get what we want, but there is always a lesson in the learning. I have learned so much from our animal friends but sometimes the lessons are very painful. I am not privy to knowing how much anything will receive in a healing, that is up to the God within.

Do you work with other animals as well? I work with all animals, dogs and cats, and give them healings as well. I have used "Young Living Essential Oils" for the last 15 years and find them wonderful to use when necessary.
For example, when I got a puppy a few years back, he ran off and got lost. Needless to say, many prayers were said since he was gone for two days. I was frantic! Happily, a very nice lady found him under her porch. He was scared to death, but happy to be found. She knocked on my door and wondered if we lost a beautiful dog and I said "Yes." And there he was in the back seat.

What happened next? I brought him in and could tell he was traumatized. They had been gone all weekend and he was under their porch. I fed him and worked on him and used peace and calming oil on him and held him for a while. He calmed down and it was a great moment when he recognized one of his Christmas toys and jumped down and started playing with it. Thank goodness he has not left again.

What keeps you busy? I do phone readings and I work on horses physically, and metaphysically by appointment. I also offer Pendulum classes and teach people how to read and understand Energy. Plus, I share with people, and educate them to use young living essential oils and be more responsible for their health and that of their pets.

You may be one of the most educated psychics in the field. Explain.
I have a doctorate in philosophy and philology from a European university since I was born in Romania. I speak Italian, Romanian, Hungarian, German, French and English. I also have degrees in Clinical Psychology, Hypnotherapy and Alternative Healing.

Did you mix your psychological counseling with your psychic counseling?
After I opened an office and began counseling people, I saw that my psychic abilities interfered with my Clinical Psychology training. So I began to focus on psychic treatment rather than psychological methodology, and combined them rather than using one or the other.

Why didn't they go together? Psychology teaches you to counsel your clients solely based on their cognitive function. But as an intuitive, I can read them entirely—their intentions, thoughts, phobias, past lives, karma, future, and more. My abilities don't allow me to remain within the bounds of cognitive perception. They force me to evaluate my clients' spiritual selves, too. I've mastered the art of combining the intuitive and the cognitive, or "bridging" the two hemispheres of the brain.

How do they then work together? I can guide my clients towards the right path using my intuitive abilities, and I can provide them with practical knowledge and tools for fulfilling their dreams through my training in psychology. The two fields, though opposite in nature and foundation, complement each other quite well.

Why have you been described as a "favorite of the fashion flock"? I counsel a number of people in the fashion industry, including designers, and people who are in the creative arts. I focus more than others on the way people dress, introduce themselves, the fashion aspect of a person that tells you their state of mind. What colors they wear, what accessories they use, how they correlate them is how they present themselves to you. The totality of that person is represented in their fashion, their style.

Does it matter what color people wear? Tiny changes in color frequencies change your life. Every color has a different frequency, a different emotion. Shifting the color combination in someone can shift their minds. I'm intuitive and determine their best colors and combinations. I believe everyone should learn how to create a better version of oneself, and color can help us to change our vibrations.

What do the different colors mean? For example, if they're wearing beige, it means excitement is missing from their lives, but there is a sense of stability. Gray doesn't attract a lot of interest. Yellow is for royalty, just a little change from beige. Pink symbolizes new beginnings. The more colorful you are, the more you are attracting people and things that will happen to you. The brighter the color, the more excitement.

Describe your work in the jewelry field. I am a jewelry designer, and my line was featured on *QVC*. My pieces were also featured in the Fashion section of *The New York Times*. I recognize the meaning behind wearing jewelry of power, which promotes a certain energy. My pieces include the Numerology Bracelet, the Karma Pendant, Circle of Life Pendant, and the Wishing Pyramid Pendant. So my jewelry helps bring the spirit world into this world.

Are you interested in politics? I have met a lot of political figures, including Hillary Clinton, Bill Clinton, Vice President Joe Biden, and Nancy Pelosi. And many other well-known people including Barbara Walters, Joy Behar, Elisabeth Hasselbeck, Whoopi Goldberg, Ben Affleck, Liza Minnelli, Deepak Chopra, Jerry Springer, Courteney Cox, Jennifer Lopez and others.

How did being a famous singer fit into your life? I released twelve records from my teenage years through my 20s, all instant hits and sold all over Europe. I first came to America on a singing contract. Singing continues to be my biggest passion and my greatest gift. In fact, just last spring I released a new music video based on my latest song, "To Be Loved By Someone." Here is the link: http://www.youtube.com/watch?v=-rL92eUYv_Y

How did you meet your husband? I was at my father's funeral. He told me from the grave to look at the name on the tombstone reserved behind his grave. I moved to New York right after his funeral, and three days after I arrived, I met a man with that same name, got married weeks later, and lived happily together for 27 years until he passed away.

How do you feel about New Age people? When I speak to a New Age group, I tell them, half of you are nuts and half of you are sane, and I can't tell the difference.

What is your background? I was born to East Indian parents in Guyana and grew up on the northern coast of South America. Later, I graduated summa cum laude in chemistry and mathematics and got an MBA. I had a successful international business that made me a millionaire before I was forty. Before that, I also worked for several Fortune 500 corporations. Meanwhile, I had a fairy-tale marriage to the princess of my dreams.

What did you learn when your life collapsed around you? My wife died in her thirties after fighting cancer for three years, leaving me with two children. Around the same time, I lost my business and all my earthly possessions. Even my car was repossessed, and I had to start again from ground zero.

In time, I realized that while I didn't understand everything that was going on or why, there was a reason for it. It was just that I didn't have all the data, and I wasn't seeing all the parts.

It was like seeing a rug being woven from the back, before you can see the pattern. And I came to realize that one day I would understand the deeper meaning—and that there would be one. As Einstein said, "God doesn't play dice with the universe." There is an order to it all I recognized that I would have to grow through life, not just go through it. And to help me do that, I would have to develop a deeper personal relationship with God.

How did you start to pull your life together? I decided that building a life was more important than building a fortune. I wanted to write, but I didn't just think about it. I had to take the necessary steps. It's like the joke about the man who goes to church every day and keeps praying, "Oh, God, let me win the lottery!" And one day from the back of the room comes this booming voice saying, "Give me a break! Buy a ticket!"

My first book, *When You Can Walk on Water, Take the Boat*, came through me via automatic writing. My second book was about my wife and family, and it was written the same way.

Describe the process of automatically writing a book. Recently, I sat down, picked up my pen, and the words *Journey in the Fields of Forever* came out. And I said, "Wonderful, flowing, what does this mean?" And that weekend I wrote the entire final draft of my third book. Throughout my writing, I felt the

64

presence of my wife right there. When I'm doing automatic writing, I always feel the essence of close ones near me. The air changes and the temperature drops a few degrees. At times there's a stillness, and sometimes I hear music.

How can you be sure that you didn't write your books? I couldn't have thought up some of those things I wrote. I've read them and said, "Wow, that's good." And maybe I did write them. If words come from deep within you or way outside you, it's all one, so it doesn't matter. How do I know where one entity starts and the other begins? I claim I wrote them, my name is on them, and I'm getting the royalties.

Do you think ESP has practical applications? There's no doubt that it saves lives. Several years ago, I was working as a production manager and deciding who was going to work on which shift. I pulled out the paper and I started saying to the people around me, "You, James, will work on tomorrow's shift." But when I went to write that in, I couldn't write it. And a strange feeling came over me that said "Cancel the shift tomorrow."
The following day, around three, I got a call saying, "Thank goodness you didn't have anyone working here. There was a horrible explosion and someone would have been killed. The fire trucks are here now."

What happens when we die? No one actually dies. If we love someone and they love us, we are always in touch. I still feel my wife's presence, and I get data from her that helps me. I also get little signs from my son of things she has said to him since she died, things that could only come from her.
Death is just beyond that door and the curtain is very thin, and every once in a while the curtain parts and we get a glimpse of what's on the other side. Once we get there, if we were terrible here, we don't instantly get transformed into angels. We have to work for it. We have to learn. It's a process of evolution in the other life.

PSYCHIC MEDIUM

RICK HAYES

lgteam@lifesgift.com
(812)556-0263
PO Box 356, Jasper, Indiana 47547
www.LifesGift.com

This psychic medium from Indiana was named Medium of the Year in 2013 by the Paranormal Awards in New Hampshire, and appeared in two docu-films on national television.

www.facebook.com/rickhayespsychicmedium
www.twitter.com/lifesgift1

BOOKS: "Stepping Stones—Thoughts Along Life's Path," "You're Not Crazy, You Have a Ghost," "Reasons for Hauntings."
DVDs: "The Possessed." (as seen on SyFy and Chiller channel)
Audio: "Your New Life Attitude."

To schedule a phone, Skype or in-person reading, e-mail
lgteam@lifesgift.com or call (812)556-0263

What was your most unusual prediction? Perhaps the time my son and I were having our breakfast watching the launching of the space mission Columbia. Everything appeared normal but I looked over to my son and shared: "They are OK, they have moved on."

He looked at me funny but within minutes we witnessed the tragedy unfold. I feel this was shared with me to know they had already transcended into their body of spirit and the explosion would not be felt.

Did a near death experience change your outlook? In my early twenties I became gravely ill which at the time we could not understand. After several days in the hospital, the doctors determined it to be a double rupture of the appendix.

I was near the end of my life on earth as per the doctors, but something was telling me otherwise. For 33 days I was in the hospital, and for several days was unconscious.

A memory of the time unconscious was receiving the vision of an angel appearing to me and sharing the words, "you will not be received yet, as you have much more to do here." At the time I could not understand the statement, but for the past 12 years—I now know.

Did you have your intuitive gifts as a child? I believe upon birth one is given many gifts, including the gift to acknowledge those in spirit and what many define as a "sixth sense."

The earliest I recall was being that of a young four to five year old child seeing and hearing those who others told me were no longer with us or had passed away.

I grew up in a church-oriented background—my grandfather was a highly respected evangelist—but I strived to keep my gifts to myself growing up. I wanted to be what I thought was "just being a normal child." Whatever that is.

How did you get started professionally? I experienced a successful corporate career, but kept my abilities hidden within. But in 2003, for the first time, I relayed messages to a friend in need.

A few days later, she came into my office and said: "Your messages were right, and because of that it brought me so much comfort. Why are you being so selfish and keeping your gifts to yourself? You could be helping others."

That night I prayed and asked for guidance, and soon began LifesGift, Inc. to follow the path of purpose.

What person did you help the most? I just received an e-mail from one who I had shared that she would be given the choice to receive a daughter. A year after the consult, she became ill with a unique and unknown disease. It affected her heart and the loss of two thirds of her hair. Although her doctor cannot explain it, she suddenly became healthy once again and soon after conceived... with the blessing of a beautiful daughter.

Do you communicate to your clients messages that seem to have no meaning? There are times I will receive a message that for me appears to be downright crazy but know to go ahead and share the message. For example in one consultation, I shared the message, "remove the thing that is on the shoulder of my uniform."

The client acknowledged her son's uniform—he had moved on in the military just a couple of years before—was indeed hanging still in his room. But it was impossible for anything to be on the shoulder as it was dry cleaned and hanging inside of a plastic bag.

The next day she sent an email and indeed acknowledged when she arrived home she went to look at the uniform. A strip of paper from the dry cleaners was draped over the shoulder of the uniform. It was hiding the medals he had been honored with that were pinned on the uniform.

Do you use any type of tools, spirit guides, or guardian angels to help you in your work? I believe tools are simply items for those in consult to see something concrete. I just share what I am to share.

I do believe in angels, which I define in one of my books as "God's Upper Management"—but I do not enhance or 'make me mystical' by sharing that I am being channeled or guided by a certain spirit guide.

That's okay for others, but I know where my abilities come from and have no need to make me something special.

Do you connect with the dead? It is routine for me to connect with those who have moved on, but I do not use the word death or dead, which means an end. We do not end in life, but simply transcend into our body of spirit and move on.

PSYCHIC
(SPECIALTY: OSCAR PREDICTIONS)

JUDY HEVENLY

Judy@JudyHevenly.com
JudyHevenly1@gmail.com
(310) 820-7280
11955 Missouri Ave, Suite 10, Los Angeles, CA 90025
www.JudyHevenly.com

She's best known for the accuracy of her annual Oscar predictions, but as a Hollywood psychic, she has read for Sharon Osbourne, Joan Rivers, Ronald Reagan, Bob Hope, Valerie Harper, Sean Connery, Goldie Hawn, and others.

www.facebook.com/JudyHevenly
www.twitter.com/1hevenly, www.twitter.com/hevenlyjudy

To schedule a phone, Skype or in-person reading, call (310) 820-7280 or e-mail Judy@JudyHevenly.com

Do Hollywood people pay psychics a lot of money? None of them ever pays. They come up in their limos. They've forgotten their purse, or they feel that you should give a reading to them for nothing. I make the majority of money from blue-collar working people. I learned there was something more than money or fame and that's your inner self. I learned to close my eyes and listen to my inner voice, the God within.

Do you have many famous clients? I have met and read for many celebrities, including Ronald Reagan, Valerie Harper, Bob Hope. Sean Connery, Sharon Osbourne, Goldie Hawn, I attended two garden parties with the Royal Family at Buckingham Palace after making accurate predictions for them. But not all of my clients are in Hollywood; some are in other parts of America—small towns that nobody can reach—but I talk with the people over the phone, and they reach me on Skype.

What are you best known for? Every year I make Oscar predictions that are broadcast all over the world. I am often 80, 90, sometimes 100 percent accurate. Because of my knowledge of the film business-I studied movie making at UCLA-and because I can help to finance movies on the side. I am able to tune in easily. Every day I get up at 4:30 to meditate and pray for my clients, but about a week before the Oscars, Oscar information is given to me. Then each year now the press calls me and I tell them what I see for the awards.

Were any of your family members in the film business? My former husband, whom I met when I left South Africa and moved to London at 18. I bought my wedding dress two weeks before I met him. He was a screenwriter for Warner Brothers working in London. He wrote the TV series *The FBI.*

With your interest in films, have you ever been in any movies? I came to the United States in 1968. I got my dream then of being in the movies— although not of being a star-when I was spotted by the man who discovered the Beatles. I ended up in a small role. And that led to another bit part in a movie with Shirley MacLaine called *The Yellow Rolls-Royce.*

Did someone help you develop your mysticism? My father was in the funeral business for a while. He came into contact with people who were dead. He was the one who taught me as a child to close my eyes and go within. Because of this experience I am able to contact departed loved ones on the other side.

Do you think your being from South Africa had something to do with your development in this area? Yes, being from a land of magic and mysticism enhanced my psychic abilities. Also, it's a simpler life there. Psychics can accept the voice of intuition. Here in America there are too many distractions that prevent you from hearing that voice.

Did you train as a psychic? I joined an institute where they had all the young up-and-coming psychics, people who later became well known. We started at five dollars a reading. If we made three or four mistakes, we were out. If we made bad predictions, those were considered mistakes. We gave thirty readings a day on Saturday and Sunday. I was guided by a very active inner voice saying to me, Tell them this! Tell them that! Now, I still use this voice and I sometimes use the angel cards.

What do you tell your clients? For most of my movie and business clients, I am like a poor man's psychiatrist, giving them predictions. Celebrities rely on what I say, but I only make suggestions, such as "Why don't you try meditation?" or "Why don't you try being more self-reliant and look for the answers within yourself rather than always running off to a psychic?"

What is your blue dot meditation? I have also become well known for *The National Enquirer's* blue dot meditation, which I also use with clients. I energize the Blue Dot for *The National Enquirer*, and I put a lot of thought energy into it. It is resulted in over $300 million for its readers. When people touch the dot, if they believe hard enough, their thoughts will make their wishes happen. By touching this dot, six people around the world have won major lotteries. One won the New York State Lottery for 2.7 million dollars, and one in California winning a $60 Mega Million jackpot.

What is the best advice you give people? To be yourself, to rely on your own intuition, and be brave enough to follow it. When my clients are trying to make a decision, I often say to them, Imagine yes in one hand and no in the other. And then ask your higher self to raise the hand that has the correct answer.

PSYCHIC MEDIUM
(SPECIALTY: FENG SHUI)

DIANE HILLER, LCSW

DianeHiller@optonline.net
(860) 601-1263

www.elementalempowerments.com

This Connecticut former nurse and social worker, is now a psychic medium and certified Feng Shui Master.

www.facebook.com/diane.hiller.56
www.linkedin.com/pub/diane-hiller/35/15/23
www.twitter.com/DianeLynnHiller

To schedule a phone, Skype or in-person reading, call
(860) 601-1263 or e-mail DianeHiller@optonline.net

What does it mean to be a Feng Shui master? I am certified as a (BTB) Tibetan Buddhist Feng Shui Master™, and also the founder of Elemental Empowerments, LLC. We are trained to adjust chi—the vital energetic force that is present in all beings and things—to its most appropriate level, to bring individuals and their environments into harmony. These adjustments may be to one's own personal chi or to a business or home environment.

How does this apply to most people? Within your home or business, there are 9 baquas or power spots. They are directly related to: Career, Knowledge and Spirituality, Family, Wealth, Reputation, Relationship, Children, Creativity and the Future, Benefactors, and the Tai Chi, or the center of yin/yang energy.

How can Feng Shui be used to improve one's personal life? Feng Shui applications can attract romance or improve an existing relationship, change or improve your career, improve your health and vitality, increase your finances, and help with the sale of a property. It can be used to enhance your business by attracting new customers, improving your cash flow, removing negative energy, and help to design enticing business cards and letterhead.

What specifically do you do to affect this? Consultations can be done at the client's space or through a floor plan reading. I make suggestions to improve the "energy" by offering a traditional rice blessing ceremony, clearing space through the use of mantra, sound, smudging, and sacred drumming. If the energy is stuck, moving too fast, blocked or absent, corrections may involve the use of color. Or movement of furniture. Or the purchase of plants, mirrors or other specially suggested objects.

Can you give examples of your cases? I had a client who was unemployed and could not find a job. I did a scan of her house. I sensed a water leak and found she had a leaky bathroom sink in her career area. She kept throwing the water outside of the house to water plants. I told her this was representative of money and career energy loss and to fix the leak. She did and within two weeks I got an email that she had three job offers! I had another client who also was having problems with getting a job. Her front door located in the career area of her home had a stuck lock so that she had to kick the door open. This is energetically symbolic for stuck career energy. I told her to replace the lock it or use some WD-40, she did. Within two days someone she had been trying to find on Linked In that she had lost track of for years contacted her to come to her aid.

73

Were your parents receptive to this? Though this is an intergenerational gift, my mother was afraid of it. She thought I would be ridiculed for it, so I shut it down. In fact, I told my mother, "Someone very important is going to die," and three days later President Kennedy was assassinated. It was not long after this that I was encouraged to not talk about my gift anymore. It was not until the age of 40 that I began to feel the push to get on my true path.

Describe your epiphany or moment of truth. It began as rush of energy while chanting, with my body going through hand gestures that I later realized were very sacred, plus involuntary mudras, which are positions of the body that have some kind of influence on the energies of the body. I am told my physical appearance changed to that of a 25-year-old woman with bright emerald green eyes for a period of about 10 minutes. I was aware of what was going on the entire time, but it was like a force of nature had come in, taken over or fully exploded what already existed. When it stopped I was prostrated on the floor with my hands above my head in full prayer position. I was asked to take a vow, to work to help those who suffer. Everyone in the room had tears running down their faces.

After studying shamanism, how did you learn who your guides were? I asked my Shaman, "What's her name?" She said, "You have to figure that out on your own." About three days later, she came to me at night with a peaceful and angelic voice as she whispered close to my ear, "My name is Carolyn." My third guide, Patti, is a departed karmic soul connection who guides me in business and practical affairs.

Do you ever turn people away? I read for all types of clients from all walks of life but I am not able to read though extreme anger. I connect with most people, but if I do not within the first five minutes or so, I refer them on and offer a refund. This happens rarely, but it does happen.

PSYCHIC
(SPECIALTY: TAROT & ASTROLOGY)

SHEILAA HITE

In2itivone@aol.com

www.SheilaaHite.com

An astrologer, tarot master, and born intuitive, she has done everything from ghost busting to love counseling to helping people get over stage fright.

www.facebook.com/sheilaahite
www.linkedin.com/in/sheilaahite

BOOKS: "The Spiritual Hedonist," "Secrets of a Psychic Counselor," "The Infinite Tarot."

To schedule a phone, Skype, or in-person reading, go to
http://www.sheilaahite.com/book-a-reading

What is your most unusual case? I once talked a woman whom I didn't know out of suicide. She called me, wouldn't give me her last name or phone number, and said, "As soon as we're done talking, I'm going to kill myself."

Did she tell you why? She was at the end of a bad relationship, and nothing had ever worked out for her. For two hours I chose to work with her, and whatever I said showed her that one person in this world cared about her and thought she was of value and worth saving. I got her assurance that she wouldn't kill herself and asked her to call me the next day.

Did she? She called to thank me and said she saw the world in a different way. I referred her to a therapist. I never did get paid. I love money and it does wonderful things, but you can't really say to a potential suicide: "By the way, do you have any money?"

Describe a haunted house you've been in. For NBC's *The Other Side*, I spent a night in a haunted inn in Gettysburg, Pennsylvania. The place had been used as a hospital and amputorium, and I felt a lot of pain and agony. As I went through the place, I felt strong presences of soldiers killed during the Battle of Gettysburg.
In the cluttered attic was the most negative energy. I saw a young, confused Confederate soldier in the corner. He was badly wounded and had died slowly and painfully for a cause he did not understand.

Were you scared? That night, when I went to my bedroom, I left the light on. I didn't want to go to sleep. I kept telling myself that I was a brave person and that I must experience sleep, but I barely slept. At five-thirty in the morning, I heard heavy footsteps between my room and the one next to me. I had left the light on, but somehow it got turned off. I don't believe that happened naturally.

Were you able to change the energy in the place? Later, I saw that the attic contained the original wood of the 1800's, which attracts spirits. I said they should sort through the old relics and clear the space up there, and when they did that, the energy changed.

How have you helped people handle stage fright? I've assisted many adults and students through exams and auditions and also helped the singer and songwriter Riva Hunter, who developed stage fright and started forgetting lyrics. Through guided imagery, I gave her the tools to get past her blocks and

76

fears and adapt to situations. She has since gone on to heal her life and create the situations she desires.

How do you help people having relationship problems? I can't solve the problems in relationships—that's up to the couple—but I can give people a different perspective and information that isn't readily available to them. Then they can make their own decisions about what to do. I also have therapists I work with—I feel psychics and therapists should work together—and I send clients to those who are sympathetic to the fact that the person is sensitive enough to seek out a psychic.

When did you become professional? I had been reluctant throughout my life to fully employ my intuitive skills, although I had used them throughout the years for extra money or as a favor to friends. But in 1988 I became full-time. I began working the fairs in Santa Monica, and in Malibu I worked at the Malibu Shaman Book Store. I now teach and consult with clients worldwide—India; Montevideo, Uruguay; Malaysia, Hawaii, New Orleans, Buenos Aires, New Mexico and Europe. Wherever I go, I wind up working, although I don't travel to work.

What did you do before? Career wise, I designed and manufactured clothing, and I was a costume designer and costumer for television and films. I've worked on *Hill Street Blues*, *Blade Runner*, and *The New Alfred Hitchcock Presents*. I have also been a waitress, an accountant, and a business manager.

What methods do you use? Since I am psychic, I can work without tools, but at different times I use tarot, astrology, psychometry, palmistry, dream interpretation, channeling, meditation, healing, and hypnotherapy. Although one of my specialties is past-life regression, I believe the life you are living now is the most important one. You want to look at it and see what's going on there.

How would you describe yourself? Ted Andrews, the bestselling author of *"Animal Speak"* and *"How to Meet Your Spirit Guides"* said of me, "At a time when everyone seems to be hanging up their 'psychic shingle,' Ms. Hite demonstrates how it should be done—professional, skilled and inspiring."

PSYCHIC MEDIUM

JOHN HOLLAND

info@JohnHolland.com
www.JohnHolland.com

This New England psychic medium, featured in "The World's Greatest Psychics," is renowned for being one of the most accurate and evidential mediums on the world stage.

www.facebook.com/JHollandMedium
www.twitter.com/jhollandmedium

BOOKS: "Born Knowing - Accepting and Embracing my Spiritual Gifts," "101 Ways to Jump Start your Intuition," "Psychic Navigator - Harnessing your Inner Guidance," "Power of the Soul - Inside Wisdom for an Outside World," "The Psychic Tarot Oracle Deck," "The Spirit Whisperer - Chronicles of a Medium."

ORACLE DECKS [coming soon]: "The Psychic Tarot for the Heart Oracle Deck," "The Spirit Message Daily Guidance Oracle Deck."

Check his website for speaking engagements, event details and up-coming workshops at http://www.johnholland.com

When did you first realize you had this gift? I always realized I was the different one in my family. As a child I was very sensitive, as I often knew when people were going to suddenly visit our home. I would see Spirit People walking across my bedroom and thought I was dreaming. I just knew when certain things were going to happen. Plus, I was also very open to other peoples' emotions and the environment that surrounded me.

Was there an acceptance of you? No, my family and society ridiculed me for being different! I was considered weird because I was always reading metaphysical books when I was a child, instead of playing outside with my brothers and sisters. I was left feeling isolated and alone because I had these unusual psychic abilities. I had to come to terms with this rare gift, and the steep learning curve, to accept and embrace my spiritual gifts as a psychic medium.

What made you accept your own abilities? I fought them for a long time, refusing to acknowledge my gift until a near-fatal automobile accident lead to a near death experience, which amplified my abilities to the point where I was forced to confront them once and for all. I had to learn how to control what I'd been constantly pushing away. Whether it was fate or pure chance, I was presented with an opportunity to take a leap of faith.

Did you have any formal study of spiritualism? I didn't discover spiritualism until my mediumship started to develop. When my mediumistic abilities started to surface, I researched books to understand what was happening to me, and much of my research referred to spiritualism. Spiritualism is simply a religion of faith that believes in the continuity of life, and that really resonated with me.

Why did you choose to study in England? Actually it chose me! I had been drawn by the history and knowledge of spiritualism there, and always wished I could go there to study. Synchronistic events began to happen. I met someone unexpectedly and they just happened to be from England, and I was invited over and took the opportunity and the signs that were leading me there. I spent a lot of time sitting in a development circle, and had the opportunity to get further training at the Arthur Findlay College, which is famous as a training institute for psychic studies and mediumship development, where I learned many of the skills I continue to use to this very day. It was a thorough grounding in the techniques. To this day, I feel honored to have been so graciously accepted and respected within this tightly knit, conservative British spiritualist community.

Have you written about some of this? Both in "Born Knowing" and my last book "The Spirit Whisperer—Chronicles of a Medium," I tried to offer readers some of my wisdom and guidance on how they could develop their own intuitive psychic abilities. I also tried to remove some of the "psychic babble" by validating and dispelling some of the mystery and myths regarding mediumship. In these books, I candidly wrote about my readings with "real life" clients, including those who've had their own After Death Communications (ADCs)—from the sometimes outrageous to the profound.

What are ADCs? They're After Death Communications, which happen frequently, even though people may be unaware of them because often times they can be quite subtle. These are signs from those on the Other Side letting you know they are still with you. They could be a dream of a loved one, blinking lights, finding shiny pennies, or even suddenly hearing a favorite song of a loved one who has passed that you were just thinking of.

Is mediumship a gift? I like to think of it as an ability. The veil between this world and the next is very thin. The people who receive a message through me from loved ones on the Other Side often tell me what a beautiful gift they've just received. But in reality, I'm the one who's received the ultimate gift. It's a chance for me to honor my soul purpose of being all that I can be as a spirit messenger to help others in their time of need.

Why do you think this is a language? When someone passes to the Other-Side, it's as though a new language has to be used. For me, mediumship is a special language that transcends time and space—a language that's not constrained by the limitations of just words—but one that consists of signs, symbols, energy, and thoughts. A language that can only be heard when one truly listens. As a medium, I have the ability to see, hear, and feel beyond that veil and communicate with the spirit world. It's the language of spirit, which is how I came up with the title of my last book "The Spirit Whisperer."

PSYCHICS
(SPECIALTY: AUTOMATIC WRITING)

TERRY AND LINDA JAMISON

www.PsychicTwins.com

The Psychic Twins from Los Angeles accurately predicted the 9/11 attacks in 1999 and have since documented hundreds of world predictions.

www.facebook.com/groups/thepsychictwins
www.linkedin.com/pub/psychic-twins/56/100/491
https://twitter.com/psychictwins

BOOKS: "Psychic Intelligence: Tune in and
Discover the Power of Your Intuition," and
"Separated at Earth: The Story of the Psychic Twins."

For a phone or in-person reading, go to web form at
http://www.psychictwins.com/links

How do you two work together? (Terry) When we do phone readings, it's a three-way call. In person, we sit side by side opposite the client. We don't double our rates. We charge less than most psychics, so people are getting two excellent psychics for the price of one! (Linda) We're two channels, no waiting.

How long have you been doing psychic work? (Linda) We have been professional psychic mediums for over 20 years.

Are you two identical? (Terry) We are identical twins—true clones! But I'm more the introvert, more introspective, a little more cautious—the quieter one. Linda is very outgoing, more of a risk taker, perhaps more flamboyant. As artists, our painting styles are very different. As psychics, we prefer to work together and we work almost identically.

What did you do before you began channeling people? (Linda) We were performance artists and comic actresses. We ran our own theatrical company for ten years in New York City, producing hundreds of fantasy themed events all over the country, as well as performing in them. (Terry) Some of our biggest events were for The White House and many Fortune 500 companies. We performed at Lincoln Center with Bob Hope and Pavarotti. For each event, we did comedy, singing, robotic mime, and designed elaborate costumes. We also starred on Saturday Night Live as Louise, the two-headed housewife!

Was your family theatrical or artistic? Our parents were watercolor masters and our father is Philip Jamison, whose paintings hang in museums. We also have degrees in painting and studied in Rome. We still paint and have a 'Psychic Twins to the Rescue' cartoon series. Our mother was a very dramatic and funny redhead, kind of like Lucy. We later became professional comedians.

Did some crisis lead to your current calling? (Linda) We both suffered from the same baffling chronic illnesses most of our lives, including fibromyalgia, cancer, depression, excruciating pain, fatigue and constant migraines that almost killed us. This catapulted us on a spiritual odyssey. By the time we reached our twenties, we were so ill. Medicine had failed us. We went on a long search to find help. We worked with a psychic healer who encouraged us to develop our psychic gifts.

How do you do your automatic writing? (Linda) We've created our own divination system using automatic writing to predict the future and describe past lives. It's a very elegant, embellished script, almost like an illuminated manuscript. (Terry) Before we begin channeling, we say a prayer of protection invoking our highest guides and angelic entities so we will receive only the clearest information through our writing. We are known as "Nostradamus in Heels." Our 9/11 prediction on radio was the biggest prophecy ever recorded.

Was there any background or training that helped you in this channeling? (Terry) We've been practicing Buddhists for thirty years. That's opened us up so much psychically.

How do you help people who contact you? (Linda) We offer guidance about what to expect in the areas of love, money, career, finance, health, and family matters. We are also spiritual counselors and healers. (Terry) A lot of people come to us with romantic problems. It is common for women to ask, "Is he going to come back?" "Am I going to get divorced?" "Am I going to marry again?" "When will I meet Mr. Right?" Women have been encouraged to put their happiness outside themselves.

And what do you do for them? (Terry) Typically, we work with clients in terms of reclaiming their own power. We help them take more responsibility for developing their lives and their talents. We teach people how to change their destiny rather than be a victim, as well as the importance of forgiveness.

Besides being twins, how do you differ from regular therapists or counselors? (Linda) We perceive specific events and traumas in someone's past that may take a therapist years to uncover. We help our clients to discover their authentic purpose in life, and the best use of their talents and abilities. We can predict future events as well as potential obstacles in the areas of love, relationships, health and money. No therapist can do this.

Can you give a specific example? (Terry) We might say, "You were abused as a child," or "Your father was withholding love," or "Your parents were absentee," and we'll be absolutely right! We're not guessing.

How do people react to you? (Linda) They seem to respond to our energy in an amazing way. We're used to speaking in front of large television audiences (ABC *Nightline*, Oprah's OWN Network, *The View, Good Morning America* are just a few). Our main thrust in the work we do is encouragement, self-empowerment and getting in touch with one's spiritual side.

PSYCHIC MEDIUM

THOMAS JOHN

info@MediumThomas.com
(347) 637-8592

www.MediumThomas.com

This 29-year-old celebrity psychic medium "has quickly become one of the most respected and sought after psychics on either coast and in between," says Showbiz.

www.facebook.com/MediumThomasfans
www.twitter.com/MediumThomas

To schedule a phone or in-person reading, go to
http://www.mediumthomas.com

What did the *Hollywood Reporter* say about you this year? In "Why Psychics Are the New Must-Have Hollywood Advisors," they wrote: "Perhaps Hollywood's youngest psychic at 28, John, who often travels to LA from his NYC home base, may also be among the most in-demand." He does as many as eight readings a day (at $300 an hour) and is booked six to twelve months in advance.

You received some very strong endorsements in that story. Yes, Jenny McCarthy told them that "I've been to many mediums but Thomas is by far the most accurate one. Spot on!" Another quote: "Recently I was trying to decide if I should buy my name back from the Japanese to distribute product there under my own banner. I spoke with several lawyers and got very mixed advice. Thomas John helped me position myself to triple my revenue."

What are some high-profile celebrity events that you have predicted? I give headlines before they happen! At the beginning of the year, I made 99 predictions on my website and blog radio talk show, many of which are celebrity and Hollywood-related.
I was highly accurate, including revealing the scoop on Tinseltown starlets such as Sandra Bullock, Jennifer Aniston, and Brad Pitt. I predicted the divorce between Tom Cruise and Katie Holmes, the custody battle surrounding Michael Jackson's children, as well as the announcement of Jessica Simpson's new maternity line.

Describe your story about the Osbournes that recently made headlines. I accurately predicted the Osbourne family's current drama. I predicted that Sharon would be "in the news for something very important—more so than just normal stuff," predicting "something major with her." Afterwards, the *America's Got Talent* judge quit the popular show because NBC fired her son, Jack Osbourne, after his recent diagnosis with multiple sclerosis—two days before he was to co-star on the network's new reality show *Stars Earn Stripes*.

What did you recently predict for InTouch for Jennifer Anniston and Brad Pitt? She will be enjoying baby bliss but for her former lover, Brad Pitt, it seems that there will be less to celebrate. He's kind of looking for a change. I feel like Angelina Jolie and Brad may be separated at some point. What I sense with him is that he has some commitment issues.

Even with Angelina Jolie? I'm picking up from him that he's kind of faking it, like he's bored. But he's sticking with it.

Does being so young help you or make people worry that you're inexperienced? When people come to see a psychic, they don't want to leave with more questions than they came with. I try to be very clear and down-to-earth in my readings. The fact that I am young means that I am connected with new trends and the latest goings on in the Facebook/twitter generation. But really, a spiritual gift doesn't have an age, gender, or cultural barrier.

Did your parents accept your gift? Initially, no, because they were so devoutly Catholic, and when I was a boy, I started telling them stuff. They took me to a shrinks, doctors, even priests because they thought I needed an exorcism.

And now? My mother loves readings now that she's gotten accustomed to me. She'll go to anyone and everyone. Her first question is always: "What's going on in my life right now?" I asked why she wanted to know the present instead of the future, and she said: "If they don't know about my current situation that they can validate, how can I trust them with the future?"

Have you ever gone to a psychic yourself? Oh yes. Every six months, on my birthday and half-birthday, I consult my own psychic, a woman in Virginia. A psychic getting a reading from another psychic is comparable to a civilian doing the same thing. I just try to stay open.

How close are we to those who have passed on? My grandmother always said, "Heaven is just seven feet above you." Our loved ones aren't that far away. And they are with us and continue to guide us no matter how many years ago they passed away. I believe that I'm merely a wire connecting the "real" world and the "spirit" world.

What do they say to us? It's a different conversation. A woman who came to me wanted to talk to her dead son and was upset because it wasn't what she expected. Talking to someone close who has passed on is not like holding hands.

PSYCHIC MEDIUM

ELIZABETH JOYCE

Elizabeth_Joyce@verizon.net
(215) 996-0646
PO Box 128, Chalfont, PA 18914
www.new-visions.com

This Pennsylvania/New Jersey intuitive has been written about in twelve books, including "The World's Greatest Psychics," where she's one of the few contemporary Americans featured.

BOOKS: "Psychic Attack—Are You A Victim?" "Ascension—Accessing The Fifth Dimension," "Ascension—Accessing The Fifth Dimension WORKBOOK," "Opening To Your Intuition and Psychic Sensitivity—Book One," "Opening To Your Intuition and Psychic Sensitivity—Book Two."

To schedule a phone, Skype or in-person reading, call
(201) 934-8986 or go to http://new-visions.com/psychic-services

You were a famous twin, right? Yes, actually, I was born one of two sets of identical twin girls. My older sisters became well known as the Toni Twins—and did live commercials on TV. My twin and I became The American Bandstand Twins, and danced on Dick Clark's *American Bandstand* for three years. I met Bobby Darin, who I later dated. I was also one of the "Leggs" girls in the 1980 commercials.

Describe a reading you did that changed someone's life. I was giving a reading to my girlfriend's mother in Ohio, who had been asking about her daughter, who lived in the state of Washington. I told her to get on a plane at once and go out there or her daughter's life would be in danger because of her husband. She went, and when she arrived, her daughter was bleeding internally, and the mother took the daughter to the hospital immediately. The doctors found she was torn apart inside. Her husband had been drugging her and performing kinky sex while she was in a drugged state. The mother indeed saved her daughter's life, and I was glad to play a helpful role in that.

Do clients always take your advice? Sometimes I will give a prediction that I know is right on, but the person/client refuses to acknowledge what they are hearing. Most times this deals with relationships, like "will he ever leave his wife?" One woman told me at the end of the reading, "Elizabeth, I probably will never see you again. You have told me the truth here, but I will not do as you have suggested. I am going to stay in this negativity. I want this married man, and I will do anything to 'get him.'" It was very sad for me. I knew she was, by choice, refusing the Light.

Do you ever predict if someone will die? No one can predict death. That is always up to God. I can predict low energy times. Also, when doing medium work or conducting a seance, I will not "call in" a person who has passed because I believe that is against Natural Law. I have the client state who they would like to hear from, and then see what happens, and who comes in during the séance session.

What did you predict about Monica Lewinsky—and Linda Tripp? One of my most famous predictions was in 1997, as follows: "A dark haired girl named Veronica will upset the White House and Clinton may not give the State of the Union address in January 1998. An angry blonde brings forth the truth, and Bill Clinton may be impeached in the fall months of 1998!" This is a time when I was glad I followed the law of never inserting words or

88

thoughts in a prediction you hear "out of thin air." I had thought the angry blonde was Hillary—but it was Linda Tripp. If I had changed the prediction, it would have lessened the accuracy. I was named "Psychic of the Year" for 1998 by *ABC News* and *The New York Daily News* for predicting and writing in *Fate Magazine* about the Clinton-Lewinsky affair more than six months before it was announced to the public.

Do you think you do anything better than what other intuitives do? Is anyone really better than another? We all have techniques and styles of reading and working with others that are on a different frequency. I do straight psychic readings—where I am streaming messages from a client's Blessed Higher Self—and I use astrology, runes, angel cards, and numerology.

Is there anything about your work in the metaphysical realm that you don't like? Rudeness! Sometimes people call and won't even give you their name. It's like they *dare* you to tell them something so they can make you wrong. Also, someone who wants to "run" the reading—and tell me what to say. That is always so funny, that people think they can dictate to God or spirit.

Do you do any work in the criminal area? Yes, in fact, in one of my dreams I helped the Texas police locate a missing elderly woman who was killed in a bizarre explosion that destroyed her home and several others. This verified story was later aired on *Unsolved Mysteries*.
Since then I have assisted the police, sheriffs' offices and FBI in finding hundreds of missing people as well. The most difficult time this ever happened to me was when I located the body of my dead stepson in 1979. Naturally, this was devastating.

Do you believe in astral travel? I always knew astral travel could be done, because I have experienced it since I was a child. The ability to travel the matrix of the universe brings us unlimited possibilities; although it's not entirely practical since I've never been able to bring home the groceries when I traveled out-of-body. Seriously, my personal out-of-body traveling has been a healing tool to gain knowledge and grow spiritually, which is a divine experience.

What's the hardest thing about doing private psychic readings? People who come to see psychics are often out-of-work people with no income, wives whose husbands are ill, women who are going through divorces or other painful transitions, and have very little money. I can't take money from them because they don't have it.

Another problem with private readings is that we are short of men in our society.

Many women go to psychics to find out how they can get their married boyfriends to leave their wives. It becomes very discouraging. So many women are dating married men, patiently waiting for them to leave their wives. They want me to tell them when it will happen. But will it really happen? In most cases, no. I cannot lie and tell them it will happen and then take money. So I don't get involved in these kinds of cases.

Besides reading for a select clientele, what do you do? I do community service radio and TV shows, guest appearances on radio and TV, freelance writing, and lecturing. I've written several books which have been published by Simon & Schuster, St. Martin's Press and Adams Media.

How did you get into media work? I started teaching yoga in my twenties. Then I went to college, got married, and had two children. I began my television show called "Trim and Slim." In it, I gave readings to telephone callers. I saw that TV put me in the position of being there for people needing help. That show led to the TV and radio shows I host today. I was able to carve out a niche for myself in the media because I am a certified hypnotherapist, and my specialties are relationships, past-life regression, dream analysis, astrology, handwriting analysis, grief therapy, and death preparation.

Give an example of the type of advice you give people on radio. A woman called me: "My father has Alzheimer's disease, and he's missing." I psychically picked up that he was in Florida. But it didn't feel tropical. I felt it was somewhere having to do with transportation and that he was sitting there waiting.

Did she find him? Later, she told her husband what I said. He reminded her that her father had old cronies living in a small town upstate. They got in their car and found her father sitting in the bus terminal in Florida, New York. No wonder I didn't see palm trees!

91

Were you brought up among psychics? My mother was a psychic who could read anything. She was a great cook and read spaghetti stuck to the bottom of the pot. She could read string beans on a dish the way other people read tea leaves! The woman was totally psychic—and I thought this was normal! She was an astrologer, and instead of teaching me to read "Run, Spot, Run," we would spend time analyzing dreams and looking them up in a dream book.

Did others appreciate your burgeoning psychic abilities? When I started school, I thought this was all terribly normal. So the first day in kindergarten, I raised my hand and told the teacher, "You have to go home now. Your mommy is very sick." She told me, "I don't want any more outbursts from you. I want you to be quiet the rest of the day." But the next day she came in with a completely different attitude toward me. She knelt by my side, took my hand, and asked, "How did you know my mother was ill? She went to the hospital yesterday." She had new respect for me!

Did you speak out after that? No, I realized you cannot just share messages without repercussions. There has to be discretion in the delivery of the message. By the time I was in first grade, I could cover my psychic abilities over completely, and people I went to school with didn't have a hint. I killed off a lot of the psychic ability I had already developed. I cut off past-life memories and invisible playmates. All that was shoved under a rug until I needed it years later.

You have strong name-recognition. Explain why. First, the radio show for the body, mind and spirit that I host has been on air since 1987 [www.am1240wgbb.com]. By the way, I do free call-ins one afternoon a week and they're repeated at www.BlogTalkRadio.com. I've also frequently been on the major talk shows like Regis—who said "Joyce just brought the house down!" Oprah, who said: "Joyce is honest, talented, fun and super-psychic!" People have often seen me on *Geraldo, Entertainment Tonight, Hard Copy, Joan Rivers*, Sally Jesse Raphael's *Sally, The Phil Donahue Show* and many others.

Is there still a strong interest in your relationship with Marilyn Monroe?
The one client everyone usually always wants to know about is Marilyn Monroe. She was a great believer in the psychic world, and I was her one and only psychic. I gave her many readings in person and by tele-phone for about eight years until her passing. Frequently, I'd pick up the phone and hear, "Hello, you, it's me." whispered in her breathy voice.

Was she a happy person? No, Marilyn was a very troubled woman. One thing that bothered her was what she was most famous for: her sexuality. She told me, "I look at other women's figures all the time. Am I a lesbian?" she wondered.

She seemed to have everything: looks, money, fame. What else did she want? Another thing that troubled her was her inability to have little people, as she called children. She had had several miscarriages in her life. She was also deeply affected by the death in 1960 of Clark Gable. He passed on shortly after filming of *The Misfits* was completed. She felt she had made him work too hard to make up for her acting, and had brought about his passing.

Do you think she committed suicide? Definitely not. She told me during a recent conversation from the other side, "I was just so tired—I never meant to take so many pills with drinks. It was an accident."

What about Lucille Ball? I was her friend for forty years and later, her medium. For Lucy, life hadn't been what she wanted either, and she was also disappointed. A few weeks before she died, she participated in a séance with me. She believed in the afterlife and made contact with her first husband, Desi, and with Joan Crawford, who was a good friend of hers.

You've been associated with John Wayne, Harry S Truman, Dwight D. Eisenhower, Rex Harrison, Lucille Ball, Marilyn Monroe, Whoopi Goldberg, Greta Garbo, Marlene Dietrich, Mae West and others. Who was the first? Some of my earliest memories are of Mae, who taught me to be clairaudient when I was about six. At that age, I was giving psychic advice to the world's most famous sex symbol!
She would call—she was friendly with my mother—and tell me to say the first thing that popped into my head, like yes or no, without thinking about it. I realize now that she was encouraging me to listen to the sound of a voice, and pick up psychic vibrations from it.

94

Do you have any mementos in addition to memories from all these people? I have a gold candelabra given to me by Marilyn Monroe, a silver candleholder from Tallulah Bankhead, a gold picture frame from the Duchess of Windsor, a jeweled throne chair from Clifton Webb, objets d'art from Greta Garbo, and gifts from many other people.

Have you been in any contact with celebrities since they've passed on? Yes, I am able to communicate with my Sweet Spirits, as I call those who pass on. When I'm in a semi-trance, I can pick up voices from the spirit world. For example, Humphrey Bogart reported to me that he was reborn as a boy in Boston, and more.

What about Elvis? Elvis's mother told me she was most upset about the wedding of her granddaughter to Michael Jackson. She couldn't understand why her granddaughter married such a freak. She also told me that the drugs and alcohol didn't kill her son. She persuaded him to join her on the other side because she was lonely, and he decided to be with her.

Have you talked to others since they died? I've even reached Jack the Ripper, but I refuse to try to contact people who died suddenly and violently like John Lennon. I try to be a gentleman. Let them rest. They've had a hard enough life on earth.

What do you think of when you look back on your accomplishments in life? So much has happened in my life, and now I can talk about it freely. In past years, psychics had to be closet psychics, but nobody thinks we're crazy today.
I'm proud of all the people I've helped personally, as well as through my books and TV performances—I've hosted my own TV series twice—and my Kenny Kingston Psychic Hot Line.

What are you proudest of? When I was considering moving to San Francisco, Marion Davies, the mistress of William Randolph Hearst, told me, "You will never be accepted in San Francisco. It's a blue blood city. It's unfriendly." And I said, "I'm going to date the debutantes and buy a house on Pacific Heights, and I'm going to master this city." And I did! But then I felt I needed new challenges and moved to Los Angeles. And when I went back to San Francisco to visit, the mayor named it Kenny Kingston Day.

ASTROLOGER

JESSICA LANYADOO

LoveLanyadoo@gmail.com

www.LoveLanyadoo.com

She's been the horoscope columnist for The San Francisco Bay Guardian for the last ten years, and was named 2013 Best Astrologer and Psychic Medium by Daily Candy.

https://www.facebook.com/JessicaLanyadoo.Astrology.
IntuitiveCounsel

To schedule a phone, Skype or in-person reading, go to
http://lovelanyadoo.squarespace.com/contact/#APPT

When did you first realize you had this gift? I had many psychic experiences, but I decided that I didn't want to be too "far out there." So I chose to focus on astrology with its tangible rules and application. I did not think I was psychic at all. The realization and integration of my gifts came in stages. For example, I was communicating with the dead for clients for many years before I trusted that it wasn't a crazy fluke. It's now a routine part of my day. My work as a Medical Intuitive and Animal Communicator has also both gotten stronger in the past ten years as I have embraced those gifts.

How did you get started professionally? I moved to San Francisco when I was 19 years old with nothing but a suitcase and a plan: I was going to work my butt off to come to mastery of astrology by the time I was 30. By then, I wanted to have a little wellness clinic and move onto mastery of Medical Astrology. And that's exactly what I did. In 2003, I started writing the weekly horoscope for The San Francisco Bay Guardian, which I am still writing today. Plus I have had a thriving full-time private practice since 1999.

Have you had any other careers or interesting jobs before this? I worked for many years with developmentally disabled adults and children. That helped me to become a more informed, compassionate and helpful practitioner to my clients, especially those who are in caretaking roles.

Do you use any type of tools, spirit guides, guardian angels to help you in your work? I communicate with my spirit guides, and I see energies in names and feel them off of objects. I am also an empath and this ability gives me great insight into medical and mental health issues. I am an accomplished astrologer, with a specialty in Medical Astrology and reading pre-natal conditions in the chart. And then I also use my trusty tarot cards as a tool to communicate with my guides and get answers to more specific questions.

What types of people come to you? I work with stock traders and clergy, teens and people in their 80's, deeply spiritual people and jaded naysayers alike! What I do does not require belief. One must only come to me with an open mind and a willingness to be a part of their own healing process, whatever that means for them.

PSYCHIC MEDIUM
(SPECIALTY: REIKI)

RUTH LARKIN

RuthLarkin3@comcast.net

www.BeantownMedium.com

This Medway psychic, known as "The Beantown Medium," in addition to private readings and public events, gives free readings to people who have lost a child.

https://www.facebook.com/BeanTownMedium www.twitter.com/BeanTownMedium

To schedule a telephone or in-person session, go to www.BeanTown-Medium.com/Phone_Readings.html

What is your background? As normal as possible coming from a very large Irish Catholic family and being the oldest of nine children. We were very religious and regularly all said the rosary together. I remember thinking that I had a calling to work for God when I was in high school, but thought my only option was to be a nun. Of course, being a normal girl who liked boys, that certainly didn't interest me!

Have you ever been surprised by something that happened while working? Being a psychic almost nothing surprises me. But once, I was investigating a home where the owners were sure they had a ghost. I found an Indian spirit who was protecting their home and gave them the history and name of the tribe. As we went through their large house, in the last room which was their master bedroom, I was greeted by two incredibly large angels. I saw and heard them move and it was the most beautiful experience I have ever had.

Do the fathers want to come to you as well as the mothers? Many times a father will say upon meeting me that he is there to support his family but he tells me he is a skeptic. I always say skeptics are welcome here, but you won't leave one, and then, of course, I smile. I had such a father who was also a brilliant engineer. I had set up the appointment with his wife so I was amazed and very touched when I received the following email from him.
"Thank you so much for taking the time to see me and my family, you truly are a gift from God. It's nice to know that Anthony is happy and that he felt no pain. I'm going to try real hard to open up my heart and my eyes to the thoughts that God had other plans for my son. It's just so painful because I miss him so much. Thank you again for all your help."

What case was your biggest challenge? It was definitely a family who had lost their father to suicide. I had to help the wife/mother, two teenage children and the father's mother...all in one session. At first, I thought "How in the world am I going to help all of these people?" as they all needed to hear something entirely different." But it worked.

Is most of your work the same? No, I find that I never know what I may be called upon that will be needed. I can go to an appointment to do a house clearing and find that the owner may need a reading and healing instead. I sometimes find myself doing a Chakra Clearing and a body scan (using my medical intuition) for someone who I find needs medical attention.

Are there any clients whom you might not expect? I am always surprised when I have clergy sitting in front of me. They never tell me who they are before the reading, but of course I tell them, and then joke and say "What in the world are you doing here—you know how this works."

What's a typical session for you? I have always been a hands-on healer but am now also certified in several energy healing modalities. Before every session, I pray to Jesus—I go directly to the CEO. I also fast before I read for parents who have lost a child. I want to be as clear as possible for these grieving parents and fasting will assist in making sure that my body is ready for Spirit. I also often offer complimentary Reiki healing sessions for the mothers/spouses who are having difficulty dealing with their loss.

Do you start a session differently than most? I take at least ten minutes before every client and event I do and explain how this all works. I try to take the magic and mystery out of psychic ability. I even have a little energy doll that I use to show how powerful human energy is.

What is the most unique thing that you can "see"? I can always tell who has had a miscarriage or terminated pregnancy. I know because I see these inhumanly beautiful children who look about four or five years old and their messages are always full of love and forgiveness (if needed). These are their spiritual children!

How do you feel about working with people who are so devastated because of the loss of a child? I always feel a great deal of satisfaction when a family leaves me feeling relieved and loved by the child or children they have lost. I know in my heart this is what I was always supposed to do. I would have gone down this road much earlier if I had known that I could really help people. I often say to my friends that I am really more of a spiritual therapist. I find myself guiding individuals and families in accepting and understanding why they have lost a loved one.

What is a Travel Psychic™? I have always helped people find the best routes, best means of transportation, and ease travel stress. In 2011, *The New York Times* labeled me the Travel Psychic™ because I save people anxiety when they are traveling.

How do you help them? As I told CBS News Travel Editor Peter Greenberg, before you travel you have to work with the dates of the trip. Clients bring me their itineraries, photos of where they're going, locations of the hotels, and more.

What does energy have to do with this? Before a trip, I look at their energy as a whole. I help give people power over their agendas when they are away from home by evaluating their personal energy in order to help them have the best trip possible.

Who seeks you out for travel help? Anyone! Some of my clients are afraid of planes, have to fly for business reasons, and want me to make sure they've chosen the right flight. One Wall Street power broker who often travels overseas sees me on a regular basis to go over his itineraries.

For example, when he was going to London and Dubai, I saw a red flag only when it came to food. I saw a picture in my mind of him with a distended stomach and told him to be careful. But he didn't listen to me, ate some bad food in Dubai and had to be rushed into surgery.

In your book, "Medium Rare," you said that as a teenager you got the name "Gypsy." Why? One Friday in class, my English teacher asked me to read her palm. A picture flashed in front of me of two white poodle puppies in a box wrapped with a red bow. I told her she would receive them as a gift. That Monday she told everyone she received exactly that for her anniversary. I was then given the nickname "Gypsy." The staff even set me up in one of the counselors' offices and I did readings for a quarter. It was donated to the school for their battle of the bands.

Why did you suppress your intuitive abilities for many years? I had a near-death experience during surgery for endometriosis. There were several minutes that I was "dead" on the operating table and they even gave me last rites. It was so traumatic to me that I shut psychic matters from my life for more than a decade while I came to terms with it.

What won't you read for a client? I won't read the same issue if a client has made no attempt to help themselves in the situation. Too many people become psychic dependent, relying on outside guidance rather than incorporating it with his or her own intuition. If we listen to our own power or intuition, it will right things for us in many areas. We don't need to keep addressing the same issues. I enjoy exploring new areas with clients.

You're an intuitive artist, and you've even developed an iApp. Please expand. I've had art shows in Chelsea, the Hamptons and New Jersey. The techie in me decided to create an app that expresses my artwork, along with a translation that allows people to be part of the process. You pick a card and hold on to the positive colors and words described in The Vibe™ It helps people connect regularly with positive energy through the colors and meanings of Linda Lauren's Energy Art™ and is available from iTunes.

Your metaphysical center seems to have everything—including ghosts! Yes, *Linda Lauren's Embracing the Universe* even includes an art gallery. But the building itself is haunted. We have had angel figurines move on their own, songs play messages that only we would understand, and people whisper when we are obviously alone. Pens have gone flying, shadows have moved, and I have seen a woman at a stove on the third floor named Evelyn who is cooking. But there's no stove there and no woman actually cooking.

Describe the work you do as a pet psychic? I have a column, "Psychic Companion,™" which explores past life connections with people and their pets, and pet consultations are still a part of my practice via Skype. I was filmed for an Irish "dogumentary" with my previous dog, Ginger.

They had me work with a dog named Cosmo who was always "dumpster diving" into trash. I saw a pink rubber ball and realized he was looking for it, from his connection in a previous life. I recommended getting him another pink ball and putting it in the bottom of a trashcan. A bit of paranormal sleight of hand worked!

INTUITIVE COUNSELOR

TONY LeROY

appointments@TonyLeRoy.com
(877) 818-2700

www.TonyLeRoy.com

This intuitive counselor uses his empathic ability to create a drawing that shows his clients what is going on mentally, physically, spiritually, and emotionally.

www.facebook.com/IntuitiveTonyLeRoy
www.linkedin.com/pub/tony-leroy/0/7aa/950
www.twitter.com/IntuitiveTony

To schedule a phone, Skype or in-person reading, call
(877) 818-2700 or e-mail appts@TonyLeRoy.com

How did you come to discover your abilities? The first experience that I recall I was the age of three or four; very young. I saw the spirit of my grandmother, who had passed. I shared the experience with my mother, but she did not believe me. Consequently, I learned very early in life to keep things to myself. My empathic ability really kicked in as an adolescent.

Do you literally "draw" people at the beginning of a session? Yes, I use my intuition to do a sketch of what is happening with the client. It's a drawing of what I "see" and feel at the time. For example, I might put large feet on a person who I think is well grounded; or a dash on an area of the anatomy, like the stomach, where I sense a physical or emotional problem.

What kind of information are you looking for when you are connecting with a client? The first thing I do is tune in to a person's soul, and ask that the soul comes in fully to a person's body. Then I see how the person's physical body reacts to it. I then do the drawing to help the client see what I am perceiving. This shows me any energy blocks. For example: how they are allowing abundance to flow into their lives, or how they may be manifesting a physical problem.

What advice did you give viewers on Dr. Oz? I discussed how to develop one's sixth sense. It's important to tune in, take a deep breath, and feel what's going on. It is also important to be receptive and open. Then you read your body's signals.

It is also important to unplug. This means to eliminate any external distractions. Once a day, turn off the phone, get off Facebook, and turn off the news. Take time for yourself.

Give yourself space so that you can hear your own thoughts, and tune into your own feelings. I meditate for an hour at least once a day. However, you can start with 5 minutes, something we can all do, and then build up. This is your time. Make it about you.

Do you use any tools? I look at a client's soul, and I feel where they are at this moment. Sometimes I use tarot cards. If there's a question of timing, such as, when something is going to happen, I like to use numerology. Mostly the spirit guides, mine and the clients', interact with me. The guides may have a message and/or an answer that the client may need at the time.

Do you encourage taping? Yes. It allows them to relax without having to take notes. They can bring a recording device to record their phone or Skype session. The recordings are great because the clients can revisit their sessions, and they may hear things that were missed at the session.

How did you get where you are today? I have been working as an intuitive counselor for over 20 years. I started very young. At the time, I was worried that people would not take me seriously. I received, and continue to receive, great responses about the work that I do. Every day I am deeply humbled and blessed that I get to do this work, which I love. I get to "hold up a mirror" to show people how they are presently, and how they can create a better tomorrow for themselves. I work in New York and Los Angeles, and I am also lucky enough that I get to travel the globe for my work.

How strong is a person's energy field that you're able to read people over the phone and via Skype? I don't know that it matters because I believe that there is no difference between time and space. I am able to connect with anyone, whether it is on the phone or through Skype. Sometimes I can do a session through email because I am able to feel the client's energy and guides. If a person has a strong energy field, it makes for an easier session.

Who has the strongest energy fields? Everyone gives off energy. People who constantly work on their belief systems, good and bad, have strong energy fields. Children have huge energy fields because they're so open. Celebrities and people who are in public life tend to have strong fields as well. That is because there is more attention on them, so their energy is more expanded. I also find that people who do things for others unconditionally, have big energy fields.

What do you like least about being so intuitive? Overall I love my work. Sometimes it can be very tiring. I am very sensitive, so when I am in a crowd I pick up sensations from everyone all around me. When I can, I try to avoid public transportation, because I can feel trapped by the impressions of too many people at one time. Yet, I have to be realistic. I do have a life, so I make the best of it.

NUMEROLOGIST

GLYNIS MCCANTS

Glynis@numberslady.com
(626) 614-9333
www.NumbersLady.com

The most famous person in the field of Numerology, she's a celebrity herself because she's been featured so frequently on major TV shows and well-known magazines.

www.facebook.com/pages/Glynis-McCants-The-Numbers-Lady
www.linkedin.com/pub/glynis-mccants/5/5a1/66b
www.twitter.com/Thenumberslady

BOOKS: "Love by the Numbers," "Glynis has your Number."

To schedule a phone or in-person reading, call (626) 614-9333 or go to http://www.numberslady.com

What is Numerology? It is a Science of Numbers that is 2500 years old, and it was created by Pythagoras, most known for the Pythagorean theorem. He taught that everything in the universe has a unique vibration—which translates to the Numbers 1 (the beginning) through 9 (the Number of completion), and attached traits to each Number. These Numbers influence everything from people, to homes, cities, states, businesses etc.

What first got you interested in this field? I went to a Numerologist after my first love broke my heart. I simply could not get over him. She explained that what was really holding me to him were the vibrations coming from his mother and sister. It was their Numbers that were very compatible to me, and *he was actually toxic to me!* Knowing this released me from my pain. I was so impressed that I wanted to share this knowledge with everyone. I began an intensive study of Numerology, and I have never looked back.

How have you used Numerology in your own life? I successfully used it to find my husband. I put an ad on a dating website saying "Numerologist looking for a man who has really got my Number." The man I met and married is also involved with numbers, but in a different way: he has a master's degree in statistical analysis. He has a very logical mind, and yet, he is amazed by my consistent accuracy when I read people day in and day out!

How did you become so celebrated in the field of Numerology? I became well-known as a result of doing five one-hour one-on-one shows on *The Leeza Show.* Since then, I've been a recurring guest on the *Dr. Phil* show, the *Today show, Dr. Oz, The Talk, Nightline, The View, Good Morning America,* and *Entertainment Tonight.* I've been written up in countless magazines, and I've written two best-sellers, "Love By The Numbers," and "Glynis Has Your Number." I was also an expert guest on *Dancing with the Stars*, and successfully predicted the winner of season four.

Besides being famous yourself, have you done charts for celebrities? Yes, I have many celebrity clients because when they get a reading with me, they know that I am not impressed with "who they are," and will always respect their privacy. They call on me for advice on various things such as picking a good day for signing a contract, a new project, wedding dates, what to name their baby—the kind of things we all care about.

Where do the Numbers you use come from? Say your birth date is 7-26-42, and you want to learn your most important number- The Life Path Number. You would break down the Numbers this way: 7-26-1942 =7+2+6+1+9+4+2=31. You need to reduce it to one digit, so 31= 3+1=4. The 4 is your Life Path Number. The 4 is the natural teacher; when you learn something new, you want to teach everyone else! Note: If your Life Path is an 11 or 22 before the final digit, that is considered a Master Number. It literally means you are here to "Master Your Life," and I cover this topic thoroughly in both of my books.

Are other Numbers in the chart important? Yes, they all give us different insights. A complete Numerology Blueprint of who you are has six Numbers. Three of these Numbers are derived from your name using the Pythagoras Alphabet chart. The other three Numbers come from your full birth date.

Have you noticed Numerology patterns in celebrity charts? Yes I have. Here are two examples:

Actors/Entertainers with a 1 Life Path do whatever it takes to get to the top. Tom Hanks, Tom Cruise, Jack Nicholson, Nicolas Cage, and Daniel Day Lewis all have a 1 Life Path. As for women, Lady Gaga is a 1 Life Path and always finds ways to get the media's attention. Miley Cyrus is also a 1 Life Path.

A note of caution: if a person abuses drugs or alcohol, no matter how promising their Numerology chart looks, they can lose it all. When a celebrity with a Life Path Number 7 dies, they often become even more famous after death. Princess Diana, Marilyn Monroe, and President John F. Kennedy all had a 7 Lifepath Number—a day does not go by that we are not made aware of them, even decades after their deaths.

How can the significance of these Numbers influence a person's life? "Knowledge is power. When you learn which Numbers are compatible, or toxic to you, you can navigate the waters of your life much more smoothly. You can create a successful business and have a healthy love relationship because it really is *ALL IN YOUR NUMBERS!*

LAURA MENDELSOHN

Laura@SpiritMediumLaura.com
(954) 465-7338
www.SpiritMediumLaura.com

This popular Southeast Florida psychic medium is host of the "Virtual Séance."

www.facebook.com/pages/Psychic-Medium-Laura-Mendelsohn
www.twitter.com/lauramendelsohn

E-BOOKS: "L.O.V.E. Your Life Abundance Method," "Channeling The Collective," "Psychic Creativity," "Mediumship Development," "Build Your Holistic Business," "Makeup Your Breakup: The Love Recovery System."

To schedule a phone, Skype or in-person reading, call (954) 465-7338 or email laura@spiritmediumlaura.com

Were you shocked when you first realized you had this gift? I did not know it until I began vocally channeling my guides at about 30 years old. One day, a reader told me my guides were trying to come through. As soon as I got home, I slammed my tiny apartment door closed, locked the 15 or so locks on it, and asked, no demanded, my guides come through.

How did you know that your guides had come through? To my shock, my head threw back and a loud voice boomed from my mouth. It did not feel like I was doing this. It felt like intelligence, separate from me, was speaking through me.

What did you do? I ran to the other side of my tiny apartment but there was no place to hide. A bit frightened, I asked again that they speak. They did. I was a natural mouthpiece for the voice of Spirit, and I knew it then. I was fascinated, amused and "hooked." The first guides came in to prepare me for my master guide. Mine, Ola, arrived about 14 days into the preparation.

Did you get validation of this? Yes, I found a book by Jane Roberts called, "Seth Speaks." In it, she explained what had happened to me through her story. Actually the same guides she spoke about were with me at the beginning.

The beginning? Did Spirit try to reach you as a child? I saw and heard Spirit as a very young child as I would doze off to sleep at night. This is when our brain waves slow down so spirit can make its appearance. I would hear the sound of people talking, which would get louder and louder, until it would suddenly stop to dead silence. Then strangers would appear to me and try to talk. I was petrified. My master guide would speak to me as well. He did not frighten me but these strange people did. Despite this, I lived mostly as a normal child except for an unusual interest in reading "Fairy Tales," well past the age of most children. I just loved the magical spiritual meaning hidden within the parables.

Did your artistic and acting talents help you develop your gift? Born of two professional artists, I had natural talent for art. When I would paint or draw I would go into another space, similar to psychic channeling. I also spent about five years in acting classes, which opened my psychic gateway further. I would "channel" the characters I portrayed in class or in productions. In this respect acting is very close to mediumship.

111

Give an example of someone you helped through Spirit. A woman called in on a radio show and I could psychically "see" her sitting in a wheelchair which she confirmed.

She wanted to know if she would get the Social Security Disability Insurance for which she had filed. Spirit told me she had filed twice before but been refused. She confirmed all of this. Suddenly her guides blurted through my mouth that she would get her money starting in four months. A few days later she wrote me elated. Social Security Disability had called her to tell her she had been approved and her checks would start arriving in exactly four months! Not only was her financial future going to stabilize, but she had discovered through this that she has intelligent, loving spiritual beings that want to help her.

How can a reading comfort someone if someone died unexpectedly? Closure is very difficult when people die suddenly and unexpectedly. One client's brother-in-law had died in a car accident. I brought him in from Spirit during a private session. He immediately revealed that he had died in an auto accident (confirmed) and that the driver of the car he was in was emotionally upset due to a family argument. This caused him to lose control of the car. (Confirmed.)

What did your client want to know? She was concerned whether he had died right away or had suffered. She knew the accident had happened at 7A.M., but he was not found until after 9A.M. He channeled right through me he that he did not die right away but rather bled to death from a wound to his neck. When the police report was later recovered, it said exactly that.

Have you found many metaphysical skeptics? Many think a psychic is psycho. I laugh at that. I am an intelligent human being who just has a talent for what I do, which is heal souls. I let Spirit help others through me. There are potential clients I turn away if they are looking for a "fortune teller" approach to this work. That is not what I do, nor do I endorse that. Yes, people come to me who are lonely, distressed, without answers, or in a crisis. But others come to me who just want to understand themselves better, heal, make better life choices, and get on their path. Fixing problems is my work.

What was the first manifestation of your gift? It occurred at my birth. I was born with a thin membrane draped over my head. This membrane, or caul, is well known in folklore. It is widely believed that those born with such a veil are destined to live in both the physical and spiritual world.

Do you recall your early spiritual experiences? I took many tiny peeks into the spirit world. These childhood glimpses of the world beyond this life had a profound effect on me. They were reinforced by startling events in my earthly life that included meeting my Guardian Angel, two near-death experiences, and out-of-body (astral projection) experiences.

What caused your near death experience? I was totally deaf in one ear and had an eighty percent loss in the other ear. I had surgery for this severe otitis meia, but turned out to be allergic to the anesthesia. When my heart stopped on the operating table, I sensed the doctor's struggling to save me.
I felt a strange detachment from my physical body, aware of sight, thoughts and sensations. I found myself outside my body viewing what the doctor was doing to save my life. My duplicate body seemed to be at peace as it watched what was happening on the operating table to my physical body. I heard beautiful music and melodious bells. My Guardian Angel emerged from the light. He looked at me lovingly and whispered telepathically, "Don't be afraid. I won't leave you."

When did your own journey begin for you? It started when God's mind said "Look into the mirror and see yourself as my image. How do I see life? How do I feel? How do I love? How do I create something out of nothing?" In my book, "Beyond Positive Thinking," I ask you to read my mirror technique! It will work for you, too.

You had a hard life, didn't you? I've been called a "barefoot psychic from West Virginia." My father deserted my family when I was three years old. I never made it past the 8th grade in school because I had to help my family by working from the time I was ten, babysitting and doing housework. Then, my husband disappeared and I had to go on welfare to support my three children. I had to quit my job because my rheumatoid arthritis was so bad. I couldn't walk. I couldn't even open a bottle cap.

How did you turn things around? In my wheelchair, I started meditating and focusing on God, reading the scripture. I recited daily affirmations ("I do not accept this diagnosis of incurable disease"). I visualized an image of myself with a healthy body, running and doing things. Six months later my arthritis went into remission

Describe the Power of Affirmations. Once we let go of old thinking—such as "I am no good," "God is separate from me," "There is no way out," they find as I did that all of these statements are sentences that keep us in bondage. Once we begin to learn the Power of Affirmations we see our lives taking on a better way of life. We must then drop all negative thoughts from the mind. Even when things look bad we must not dwell upon the bad. We must instead see the good things that are being done for us right now.

When did you first experience an awareness of God? I was about three. I don't believe I really understood what this feeling was. But I felt a magnetic attraction toward something that was pulling me towards the teachings of this man named Jesus. It was during this age of my life I had my first angel experience

Describe your first angel experience. I remember lying there in my bed with my eyes closed when all of a sudden I felt someone sitting down on the edge of my bed. When I opened my eyes, sitting on my bed was a man with the most beautiful eyes and face just staring at me. I did not feel he was a stranger, because in my mind I knew him. His hair was long and brown and I do not remember what he wore. But I do remember the words he spoke to me.

What did he say? He said," Patty"—the name I was called then—"I am always with you. You will never be alone." He touched me on my face and I knew everything was okay. I knew I was loved. I closed my eyes with a smile on my face and I fell asleep.
As a child I would sit and look up at the sky and wish to return back to a place called home, to return to God. To be with this man called Jesus about whom I was being taught about in Sunday school. It was like homesickness, except that it is not a sadness. It was a knowing deep in my memory of a time and a place I once lived. It was my home!

PSYCHIC MEDIUM

VICKI MONROE

Vicki@VickiMonroe.com
(207) 499-1089

www.VickiMonroe.com

This Maine spirit messenger is also a psychic medium and cold case file investigator.

BOOKS: "Understanding Spirit; Understanding Yourself," "Talking to Heaven." CD: "Voices from Heaven."

To schedule a phone, Skype or in-person reading, call
(207) 499 -1089 or visit http://vickimonroe.com/services

Did you consider yourself to be a normal child? No, I first noticed my unique abilities when I was three and turning four. I was seeing the deceased in a beautiful way. They're like angels if you want to call them that, but without the wings. These are spirits, souls, who are "in the light," and are around each of us to help aid us through life, They never frightened me, or scared me, and at that young an age, I thought everyone could see them too.

Why do you think this happened at that specific time in your life? I had just been to Disneyland, and of course I went to the Magic Kingdom. I think I identify with Tinker Bell. Of course, unlike her, I can't fly—except when I dream—but even so, I think I was seeing things through her eyes.

Were your parents supportive? Well, they took me to Disneyland. Seriously, when I occasionally mentioned what I was seeing to my mother, and she was the only one I told, she would nod and never said that what I was seeing wasn't real. I think she had an idea of what was transpiring as she had known my great-grandmother, who was a seer as well. She scared the bejesus out of me but my gift came through her. My mother realized I was just like her when she found me trying to touch the spirits I was seeing and communicating with them.

What do you see? I am like a high-resolution camera who can see those who guide others. We all have many guides who help us with the different facets of our existence. Some of the guides are people we know from this lifetime who have passed on and have made the transition back to the spirit world. Others are souls who did not exist in this lifetime but have been with us in other lifetimes, or at least have been with us in the spirit world between lives.

What happened when you came out of the psychic closet? I confided about these visions only to my mother until I was in the 6th grade. That was the first time I ever spoke out about what I was seeing. And when I did, I was suspended from school! That was my, as Oprah would put it, "aha moment!" After that, I kept what I saw to myself, and until it was apparent I was never going to have a job where I wouldn't see them. I decided to stop running so to speak and start listening. Now, I am completely "out."

Describe a case you did for _Psychic Detectives_ on the Discovery Channel. A woman disappeared in Maine and the head police detective called me. I gave him the information I received through the spirit of the person who had crossed over and come to me, which were two names that turned out to be incredibly close to what I said. I also received an odd message: "hurry and find my body before the snow falls." The detective found her just before the first snowfall.

Did you have any interesting non-psychic jobs? Oh lord! I have been a waitress, a fitness instructor, I worked for a day in a bakery. I had gotten my Certificate as a CAN and worked in a nursing home. I was a substitute teacher, and a cheerleader I was a mechanic and changed oil filters and aligned tires. I've worked as the caretaker of a beautiful historic beach front farm and their 22 homes. After I was married and had children, I then went to school to become a Certified Health Care Practitioner of Herbal Medicines. I have a PhD in that.

Were your intuitive skills active during all these many unusual jobs? Even after all of the jobs I tried, I never escaped the spirits who would find me in the grocery store, or the gyms, etc. I have tried to be many things, but I have always been psychic.

How important are these spirits in our lives? I believe that this earthly existence is a temporary place of learning and growing. It's a little like going to school. When we die, our souls leave this earthly life of fleshly confinement to go home where we feel free and liberated in the surrounding comfort of the creator's light and love.

How do these spirits contact you? Many ways but one way I receive messages from the spirit world is through sensations in my body. For instance, if a spirit wants me to know that they died from pneumonia but they can't describe it verbally, I might feel pressure in my lungs and a sensation of suffocation.

Do you work abroad? Yes, I travel extensively around the world doing lectures, teaching, and live sessions for people. I hear the messages in English, but an interpreter then translates for the local people.

PSYCHIC

LLORRAINE NEITHARDT

lln@nyc.rr.com
(212) 757-8914
353 West 56th Street Apt 2B, New York, NY 10019
www.LlorraineNeithardt.com
www.blogtalkradio.com/lneithardt

A cosmic cobbler famous for focusing on people's souls, she also works on people's soles as a famous shoemaker.

www.facebook.com/Llorraine.Neithardt
www.linkedin.com/pub/llorraine-neithardt/23/401/89a
https://twitter.com/VenusUnplugged

To schedule an appointment, call (212) 757-8914 or go to
https://booknow.appointment-plus.com/3nr21cjs/10

Tell us about your unusual background. My father raised homing pigeons on the rooftop in the Bronx. My mother's Celtic intuition knew her seventh child would bring luck and my destiny to have second sight was a given.

Did you expect to become a psychic? No. After graduating from Parsons, a friend insisted I go to a "psychic" to reveal my destiny. Then fate entered my life and turned it upside down and inside out. The psychic announced my fate as if it was the Oracle of Delphi; I was to become a Seer. I thought she was quite mad. I found out later I was mad and she was absolutely fine.

How was Shoe Art born? In the 1980's I was making one-of-a-kind evening dresses for private clients. But the clairvoyant gift demanded to be honored. So I left couture and entered the realm of consciousness. In 2004, recuperating from a near fatal car accident in Morocco, I began editing my closet, finding long forgotten earrings. Something deep in me knew these jewels were meant to adorn shoes.

Is that when you made your first step into shoes? My inner voice said, "I want to learn to make shoes." The next day I saw a notice about shoemaking classes. I took the hint. As if blessed by St. Crispin (patron saint of shoemakers), I was a natural. I created Shoe Art. I began making one-of-a-kind shoes with unusual and rare products, giving them names like "Imperia," "Papal Bride," Royal Jelli Jewel," calling some "sexual fairy slippers." [See https://shoefineart.com] My first art exhibit was "The Erotic Life of the Foots: From Soul to Soulier." I designed and made the shoes that ended up as the centerpiece of the movie *PS I Love You* with Hilary Swank.

What do shoes (soles) have to do with the soul? Shoe art is as much of a spiritual practice as meditation or the complex task of individuation. All life is interrelated. If you dream of shoes it means how you walk in life, your position or passion or how we touch Mother Earth. The symbolic meaning of shoemaker characterizes an individual who has the capability to guide the life path of others.

How do you reconcile the two interests? Now I am a psychic by day and a shoemaker by night, a part-time shoe guru unleashing the shoe within. But as a psychic, I mentor my client's souls, and I'm also radio show host of *Venus Unplugged: A Virtual Heartbreak Hotel.*

Do you ever predict disasters in a client's life? Not as an absolute but to guide them to seeing life differently, to face what life is giving them. To mature and become who they are meant to be. Whole. Strong. Beautiful. People have more inner resources to handle crisis than they realize because when something bad happens, their lives don't fall apart. They just kind of break into these different pieces to be reordered like a kaleidoscope.

Do you tell clients what to do? They must choose for themselves. A woman came to me and I saw that there was a great likelihood that her aged mother would not live through Christmas. I suggested that her mother was in an ending cycle and she might want to visit her rather than attend a holiday gala in other city. The choice was hers. She chose the gala and her mother passed on at Christmas. This woman lamented and cried and asked why didn't she see what I was saying. Through her bitter tears she learned to love, forgive and connect to her spiritual nature. Eventually she could feel her mother's love from beyond the veil. I do not give an absolute, since free will and no interference is the law of the universe.

Do you record your sessions? I digitally record and email an mp3 file after the sessions. I encourage the clients to listen to the session. Often a client will call a year later and say they listed to the session and are astounded. I am not concerned about being right or wrong, that's ego. I am concerned about what events mean to them and to the depths of their soul being. Sessions are like poetry. When they hear them at different points and at different levels, there are deeper meanings.

How do you feel about skeptics? I don't care because you can believe or not believe in electricity, but you get shocked if you stick your finger in that socket.

Do you use any tools? Metaphysics, esoteric laws, dreams, myth, archetypal psychology of C.G. Jung, language of the stars and tarot are what I use to inform my gift of clairvoyance.

How do your readings change people's lives? I mirror the deepest part of their being and mentor their soul, the parts they cannot get to. They need to have meaning to this darkness because we can suffer anything if it has meaning, and then they can start making tremendous changes. Otherwise, what we don't know about ourselves will return to us as fate. Positive change is an inside job.

PSYCHIC

BARBARA NORCROSS

Barbara@NorcrossBarbara.com
(561) 626-7101

www.NorcrossBarbara.com

Called the Palm Beach Celebrity Psychic, she received world-wide fame when she was called in on the William Kennedy Smith rape case.

https://www.facebook.com/barbara.norcross.77

To schedule a phone or in-person reading, call (561) 626-7101 or go to www.NorcrossBarbara.com/contact-barbara.html

Do you use any props? As far as I am concerned, crystal balls, Ouija boards, black cats, and Friday the thirteenth are Halloween stuff. I'm not a fortune-teller. I don't speak to the dead. I hear some things and see others. And I don't levitate anything but me.

What was your life like before you were a psychic? I've had a colorful life. One of my husbands turned out to be a gangster and not the businessman he told me he was. Another gave me a yacht as a wedding present. After our honeymoon, he disappeared for a year. Then he returned—and took the yacht!

What kind of jobs have you had? I was once a veterinary assistant. A dog groomer. A professional entertainer signed with the William Morris agency. I owned and managed two nightclubs in Texas. I was an antique store assistant, an executive chef in El Paso, Texas. I was so inundated by work that one day I asked myself, "Oh, God, how much longer do I have to do this?" That day I fell and hit stainless steel on my way down and was severely injured.

What happened after your accident? I had to learn how to walk again, and I regrouped my whole life in the seven years of surgeries. That's when I realized I had the time to dedicate myself to my psychic studies. I think God tells you things.

Were there any other incidents that changed your perception of yourself or the world? Later, when I was married to a military man and we were living in Germany after the war, I visited Dachau and went into the shower room where the Nazis had gassed prisoners. When I stepped inside, I could hear every voice of every person who ever crossed over there. I lost it. I woke up hours later in an infirmary on a military base where my family had taken me after I collapsed. After that I simply couldn't ignore my psychic abilities.

Tell us about some of your accomplishments. I have been practicing my gift for over 30 years, and have done select readings for clientele which has included Donald Trump's Mar-a-Lago Club in Palm Beach for seven years. I've been on shows like *Montel Williams, 60 Minutes, Hard Copy, Ricki Lake, Larry King,* and *Dateline.* I also had my own award-winning radio show.

Weren't you once licensed as a psychic? That's unusual. Yes, several years ago the Town Council in Palm Beach voted unanimously to issue me a license. I was the only psychic ever approved on the island.

What type of events did you do at hotels? In addition to my private clients, I did 21 years of events in the Leopard Room at the Chesterfield. For seven years, I also held "psychic luncheons" for weekend "Psychic Getaways" at the Colony Hotel. I was called the resident psychic, and they didn't have enough room to hold the crowds I brought in.

Describe your celebrity cases, such as the Kennedy and Jon-Benet Ramsey cases? I consulted on the Jon-Benet case, but I got the most publicity on the Kennedy one.
When I moved to Palm Beach in 1991, as soon as I got there, I knew something was coming down with a politician in town. Then the William Kennedy Smith scandal broke, in which the nephew of JFK, RFK and Ted Kennedy was accused (and exonerated) of raping a woman in Palm Beach. I was called in twice by one of the investigators.

What did you tell them in those two cases? If I told you, I would never be asked to work on another case by them.

Give some examples of your abilities. For example, I advised a mother not to let her son accept a ride on a particular day. Two days later, the mother called to tell me some friends had offered her son a ride, but he had turned it down at her insistence. All the kids in that car were killed right after they drove away. Another time a lady called me to say she had lost two gold rings. I saw a carpet and asked her if someone she knew had carpet installed recently. Several days later she called me back to say the rings were found under her daughter's new carpet.

How do you feel about your special ability? It's a gift from God, and I want anyone who needs a reading to be able to afford it. I've done many readings for free.
I've turned down large fees because I believe my gift must be shared. Otherwise it will be lost. As long as I use my gift to benefit others, I'll have it.

ASTROLOGER
(SPECIALTY: CHILDREN'S CHARTS)

DABNEY OLIVER

astrology@Astrocutie.com
(585) 472-4338

www.Astrocutie.com

She specializes in astrology readings for children, and is known as
"Astrocutie."

www.facebook.com/Astrologychildren
www.twitter.com/Astrocutie

To schedule a phone or in-person reading, call (585) 472-4338,
or email astrology@astrocutie.com

How does reading a children's astrological chart differ from a regular one? I look a lot more at the positive potential and recognize that the child has a whole life ahead of him or her. When you look at an adult's chart, they have a lot of baggage. And you can talk about that because adults are more accepting of their foibles.

Are there things you won't tell parents about their children's charts? Parents don't want to hear anything bad about their child, because that's their baby, and you don't want to scare them or label the child or put him or her in a box.

I wouldn't tell a parent negative or challenging things that might happen to the child. I try to focus on "Here are some of your child's strengths and here's the best way to support them on their journey." I use astrology as a guide to the best possible life they can have.

Give an example of a reading where the child's chart showed negative traits. I had a child whose chart showed he may not grow up to be the most empathetic adult. It wouldn't necessarily come naturally to him. I offset that by telling the parent they had to help their child understand what it's like to be in someone else's shoes and emphasize the other's experience.

Do you read newborn charts? I tell mothers of newborns: "Call me back when your child is six months old." Until then they're just sort of lumps looking around and the mother is just way too tired to process. But you have a sense of a child by six months old. Whether they're sensitive or playful, you can see their personality emerging. Then the parents are much more ready to hear how they can support this baby.

Give an example of how reading a child's chart helped the parent? I had a Mom who cared a lot about appearances, and she was very popular. But the daughter was being made fun of in school, and didn't have friends. And the mother's heart kept breaking for her child. But the more I talked to the mother and the child and dug into her chart, I came to realize that there was a disconnect, because the child was more upset over her mother's reaction than she was over not having a ton of friends. She didn't care what others thought of her. I showed the mother how the little girl kept trying to please her and she wasn't being herself.

126

Since the children don't pay you, how can you make money doing children's charts? During the day I work in public relations and I also write for magazines. But I realize that my path is not to make a lot of money in this line of work. It's a real challenge but I love doing children's parties. I do a lot of them, as well as parties, showers, and store events. I'll set up camp and do 15 minute readings. What's especially nice is that some have been afraid to get a reading because they're worried that someone will tell them they have a curse, or they're afraid someone will tell them something bad. So this opens a doorway for them. It shows them it isn't all voo doo hoo doo.

Have you ever personally had a bad reading? I was in my 20's and was having a hard time with a broken heart. And the reader hadn't prepared and was very casual and nonchalant about my problems. She pulled out my chart and said things like: "Oh you're a cancer, you like to decorate." I believe that when people come to you, you have a responsibility. I don't have a PhD in psychology, but this is my form of counseling people and trying to get them the best way to get to the next stage of their lives.

Do any men (or fathers) ask for readings at children's parties? I find that a lot of men are more likely to get a reading from an astrologer or a psychic if they're at a party and it's free. Then the wife or girlfriend will encourage them. Afterwards: every man I've done has said: "Wow this is interesting."

How long have you been interested in astrology? I have loved it since I can remember. I can still tell you the signs of all my best friends from years gone by. At the age of ten, my allowance was clearly allocated for the little star scrolls you could buy in line at the grocery store.

Are there people you don't enjoy working with? I sell gift certificates, and sometimes people give them to people who themselves are not open or interested in a reading. You can't force a reading on someone else—even though they intended it as a loving gesture. I also don't enjoy working with people that are looking for me to predict their exact future from their chart. I don't do that. I can help people find themselves but not necessarily their runaway pet.

PSYCHIC

KAREN PAGE

info@KarenPage.com
(213) 955-1760

www.KarenPage.com

A professional psychic for over 40 years, she has used psychometry to work with everyone from homicide detectives to members of British Parliament to Japanese media, bankers in Brazil, world-famous entertainers, politicians, housewives, and more.

BOOKS: "My Life Across the Table: Stories from a Psychic's Life."

To schedule a phone or in-person reading, call (213) 955-1760 or email info@KarenPage.com

Why were you once called "The Psychic Baker"? My husband helped design and build a boutique bakery in Beverly Hills. Then the owners decided they didn't want it. So I ended up knee-deep in flour and sugar for this unexpected chapter in my life, waking up at 1 or 2 in the morning to prepare. We called it The Banana Bread Box and people loved getting freshly baked chocolate chip banana bread with their readings.

Have any of your clients shocked you? Yes, I often find that people are not who they represent themselves to be. For example, a beautiful very wealthy married socialite came to me. She said she was happily married, but I saw a man clear as a bell in a reading and it wasn't her husband. I told her that I saw that they were having an intimate relationship. She admitted it was true—and it was her priest! As if that wasn't shocking enough, she was having a three-way relationship with him and her husband. She came to me not out of guilt but sadness that the priest wanted to stop the relationship! I told her that if she truly cared about him, she should let him go back to the life he chose. And then she wanted to know if I saw her finding anyone else to have a three-way with!

Do you use any objects for your reading? Yes, it can be a piece of jewelry, keys, something the person has worn for a year or more, a photograph, or business card.

How important is your gift in your life? The information I know about people and their lives has always been like breathing for me, or knowing what color my eyes are. From the time I was young, I could never open my mouth without some prediction falling out. I've even read for other psychics.

What was your first prediction? We lived across the street from a seemingly happy couple. But I was looking out at their beautiful home and said to my mother "Mommy, he beats his wife." My mother told me not to say things like that. But three weeks later, an ambulance pulled up and she came out with bandages on her face, and two policemen came and handcuffed him. After that, she never admonished me again.

Did you ever have any physical changes that accompanied your psychic insights? For many years, I experienced what I now call "breakthrough headaches" which could last for three weeks. After every one, some new element or part of my gift would open up within me and present itself. I feel these headaches are God's way of saying: "Pay attention, Karen."

Do you have any advice for people handling difficult issues? Yes, as I say in my book "My Life Across the Table," and in my frequent appearances on *The Morning Show with Regis Philbin* and other shows, I believe 20-40 percent of our lives are fated and absolute and will occur. But the rest is free will. So if a client asks me about something that is not fated, I tell them to go ahead: take that job or buy that house or go out with that person again.

Do you tell someone something even if it's very painful? My job as a psychic is not to pick and choose what I tell a person. The information in a reading is to help them and not mine to keep. Some of it is what I call it "a slap and a kiss." That's when I share something very painful or difficult with someone but something positive or enlightening can be born from the pain. Telling them gives them the opportunity to heal their heart, and to consciously resolve whatever issues they have been holding on to regarding the person who is leaving.

Give me an example. I once advised a woman whose husband was just retiring to take a trip in July to Italy for a month, which they had always dreamed of doing. But she went to an astrologer who told her to do it in September! I saw that he wouldn't be around in September, and felt compelled to tell her because the trip was so important to them. In September, he died of a massive heart attack, although he had appeared to be completely healthy. If they hadn't listened to me, they never would have had that final trip together.

How do you feel about clients taping interviews? I want them to. It's a reference tool so they can go back and clarify the difference between what I actually said and what they thought I said. There's a difference between what I say and what the client wants to hear. Often a client will just dig in their heels and choose not to hear what I have said.

Do you ever plan to retire? I've done readings for 40 years. If God ever no longer wants me to give readings, and wants me to, say, become a housepainter, I promise you I will be at Home Depot buying brushes the next morning.

What did you do for the movie crew in *The Butcher's Wife*? The movie is about a housewife who is a psychic. I kept up the psychic vibrations on the set. I did a lot of readings. I taught the cast members to understand and not to be afraid of psychics. I wanted them to know what it felt like to be psychic and to be read by a psychic. I read for everybody but Jeff Daniels. His part was an unbeliever in the film so we had to keep him an unbeliever.

What was your relationship with Demi Moore? I was in the trailer with her for three months, training her how to be a psychic. I wanted her to experience what it was like to give a reading so she could read for the movie. I did meditation exercises with her to help her tune into her psychic frequencies. She could make a wonderful living as a psychic.

What did you do with the movie *Ghost*? I worked strictly with the producer. She was a client, and she would come to me about her projects. I did not work with the actors.

How did you get the job working on the movie? Through the producers; they came for a reading, and they started talking about a project. Then the director came by himself, and he did not know the others had come to me, and they didn't know he had. When they asked me to work for the movie, I said, "It is time for the psychic to be out of the closet. I will do it if it will become public. I don't want to be behind closed doors anymore." I am the first psychic to ever receive an on-screen credit. I was called a psychic consultant.

It's been written that you not only read for Demi Moore, but Kim Basinger, Mary Steenburgen, Vanessa Williams, Irene Papas, and others. Is it true? I cannot say it, but they say it. That's why the stars see me; because I don't talk about them. I read for everybody, not just stars. I have many regular clients from word of mouth, too.

What are some other high-profile things that you've done in the metaphysical area? I was consulted by the Department of Justice and the Department of State on the Josef Mengele case. I had a lot of involvement in trying to get the people out in the Jim Jones case. On the Hillside Strangler case, I gave them a description, and said there were two people instead of one, which everyone was saying. And I said they were grease monkeys, which was true, and I described the identities and the addresses to the police department of things that would occur, and they did.

132

Do you consider yourself a mind reader? No, I read frequencies. Just reading another person's mind makes for a great Las Vegas act but you cannot predict anything that way.

A good reading looks to the future and gives you warnings. It offers advice on how to manipulate the future so nothing bad should happen. I give someone the choices as I see them because I am not a fatalist. We do have choices.

I tune into the person's frequency and pick up the wavelength. When I pick up a piece of jewelry, I read the waves.

Are there any clients you've turned down? A Colombian man brought me two hundred fifty thousand dollars in a bag and asked me to find his brother, whose plane was missing. I told him I couldn't take his money because the plane had disappeared into the ocean and his brother could not be found. Then the man's mother came to me and begged me to find her son. And I said, "Listen. It cannot be done." I'm a mother who lost her child and I don't want to hurt any mother. I have to tell them this: I cannot bring him back.

How do you feel about being wrong sometimes? I do not play God. I am open to being wrong. I told one girl that her husband was going to give her a gold Cadillac for Christmas. She told me, "No, Maria, he gave me one last year." I said, "But this year, he will give you an *antique* gold Cadillac."

When did you learn you were psychic? I came to America at eighteen. Then I owned a beauty salon in Los Angeles. After I visited a psychic, she told me I was psychic. I said, "Isn't everybody?" If you have a soul, you're psychic. We go to the closet in the morning. Which dress to wear? We're talking to the psychic part of us. If everyone recognized his or her own talents, I'd have a lot more professional competition. When people ask me, "Maria, why should I develop my psychic ability?" I say, "You use it for everyday living so you get more mileage out of life."

PSYCHIC HEALER

PAM RAGLAND

(949) 734-0374
www.PamRagland.com/ContactUs

www.AimingHigher.com

Although not a crime psychic, this psychic healer recently received worldwide publicity when she found a missing boy after 1,000 searchers had failed to find him. Here's the story.

www.facebook.com/pamragland
www.linkedin.com/in/pamragland
www.twitter.com/PamRagland

To schedule a phone or in-person reading, go to
www.ITuneInForYou.com

What did you do in the Terry Smith case? In two hours I found an 11-year old autistic boy who had been missing for four days. More than a thousand searchers--and dogs--looked for him in that time and I found him right where they had already looked. I went right to the partially buried body, and as a result I was a suspect though I was later cleared. A 16-year-old family member was arrested on suspicion of murder.

Did you immediately go to help when you heard about the case? I am a single mom who supports us. It was an hour and a half away. And, I realized I would have to end up publicly admitting I'm intuitive. But, I trust my intuition implicitly and there was no question, I had to go.

Did you have any help in finding him? When I got there, it was night and most of the searchers were gone. I did not know where Terry or his family lived. Since we were told he was lost, the last place I'd think he would be is at his home. I told the searchers left not to search the city "He's not there." They asked "Where is he?" I looked up, and physically turned my body to face the store and said "He's behind the store." I didn't know his home was back there. I was told "Hundreds of people have already searched there." I insisted, and we found him.

Have some people been negative about what you did? There are skeptics who would deny seeing a UFO if it landed in front of them. Frankly, I don't understand anger or jealousy directed at me for finding a missing child. It was a tragedy, and should be treated respectfully. I just went there to try to help find what I hoped and prayed was a live boy, very close in age to my own two kids. We all thought that, and it was the only reason I took my children. I certainly would not have put my kids through that if I thought I'd find a child who wouldn't be alive.

Despite your success in finding this boy, do you still avoid work in this area? Every form of intuition is like a distinct language. I know like the back of my hand why people do what they do--what drives their challenges and behavior. But, do I know the language of missing people? I would say it's like learning a new language, and I'm still learning it.

PSYCHIC

BEATRICE RICH

BeatriceRich@aol.com

www.BeatriceRich.com

She's as gifted an artist as she is a psychic.

To schedule a phone or in-person reading, call
(212) 989-1339 or email beatricerich@aol.com

You were quoted in *The New York Times* as turning people away. Why? I try not to tell people what to do. It's not my place to say "You must do this, you must not do that." In fact, I discourage some clients from coming for readings more than twice a year. More frequent sessions, and some will become too dependent on me.

Do certain objects work better for psychometry? I ask people to bring an object, such as jewelry, a pen, or a lipstick, to their session. The item cannot be an antique, a gift, or anything owned by anyone else or that they've loaned to someone else. They had to have bought it for themselves, and it must have been in their possession for at least one month. Also, it can't be a handmade object because then I might be picking up on the person who made it, rather than the one it belongs to.

Do you use anything in addition to psychometry? I almost always use a regular deck of playing cards to begin the process of getting information. The cards themselves have no intrinsic meaning. I could probably do it with chicken bones. They are a point of focus and concentration for me and for the client.

Give some examples of your telepathy. Once I got an image of a plump woman in a blue dress. She was smiling and happy, but I could only see her from the waist up. I found out later that she was in a wheelchair after being injured in an automobile accident. On another occasion, when I was reading for a young woman, I told her she was in love with a married man who had two children. She heatedly denied the fact. But I described him to her. She later called me with her apologies. The man she was seeing never told her he was married, with two children.

What was your most uncomfortably accurate prediction? When I was reading for a woman whose boyfriend worked for the CIA, I elaborated on many of its activities. The woman recorded the reading and played the tape for him. He was startled at its accuracy and wanted her to destroy the tape to protect his private missions. She talked him out of it.

Have you ever known something the person would rather you didn't know? Someone once brought a friend to me who was a professional football player. Although he walked perfectly, I saw that he had a bad knee and asked him about it. It was public knowledge, so he wasn't impressed. But then I said to him, "You're also having trouble with your other knee." He was really shocked—and upset—because he hadn't told anyone, since he didn't want to jeopardize his contract negotiations.

How did you become involved in psychic phenomena? In the mid 60's, when I was young, a friend and I went to a Gypsy tea kettle place for tea leaf readings. The sweet little old lady told me a long story about a man I would meet: He would be dark, wealthy, liked boats and motorcycles, and I would marry him. It hit me afterward that the reading had to do with a/friend in Florida, not me. I contacted the friend, and she married him soon after. After this experience, I said to myself, "I can do this," and began studying the process. I bought cards because I am not crazy about tea.

Have you ever seen a spirit or apparition? Yes, usually connected with people I am reading for. They appear like smoke. I describe them to the people, and they turn out to be their relatives who have departed. I had one terrifying experience with one. I was meditating in a pitch-black room and heard a deep, raspy male voice gasping behind me. I turned on every light, but no one was there. It took an hour for the sound to subside.

Have you ever experimented with Ouija or séances? Yes, but now I am more cautious and will not do it again. The scenes were like something out of a horror movie. There were raps and taps, and the table would lift up and bang down. It often felt like something was shooting inside the table. Heavy chairs and tables that normally took two men to lift rose easily.

Is there a reason that you don't use Ouija boards any more? I realized that I could tap into something undesirable. There are elements we are not aware of that should be left alone. Some things beyond our dimension could possibly be harmful. I became curious as to what was happening and thought maybe it was collective energy or that we were tapping into another dimension but I never figured it out.

You're also well-known for your artistic work. I've always been a painter and sell paintings privately. I've written and illustrated several children's books, including popular books on angels ("Vanessa and the Angel" and "Vanessa and the Enchanted Painting,") which introduces children to the spiritual world in a non-denomination way
[Note: see www.beatricerich.com/books.html]
138

ASTROLOGER

IRIS SALTZMAN

IrisSaltzman@yahoo.com
(954) 986-1303
Iris Saltzman Center, 12289 Pembroke Road, Mailbox #70
Pembroke Pines, FL 33025
www.IrisSaltzman.com

Esquire called her, one of the top astrologers in the country, and she's now an intuitive astrologer with her own school, the Iris Saltzman Center in Pembroke Pines, Florida

BOOKS: "Many Lives, Many Masters" by Dr. Brian Weiss
(features Iris Saltzman)

To schedule a phone or in-person reading call, (954) 986-1303 or email IrisSaltzman@yahoo.com

How can astrology help people determine their own destiny? For example, children born at the same instant will all have the same ability to carve. One might become a surgeon; a second, a butcher; and the third a murderer. Family influence and abilities play a big role.

When did you realize you were not just an astrologer but an intuitive one? When I saw I could do astrology without knowing the person's birthday. Even if they gave me the wrong day, month, and year, I would be able to give them a perfect reading. My psychic ability was correcting the wheel! It really started blowing my mind.

How do you combine your psychic talents with astrology? For astrology, I use the left side of my brain, the one of the logical world and everyday activities. And for the psychic world, I use the right side of my brain, the visual portion. I use them together, which is supposed to be unique, although I find it natural for me.

Do we still have the primitive in us? Man has gone too far from his beginning. We're too involved with left-brain activity. I believe everyone has right-brain potential and is psychic, but haven't developed it. I've developed mine more. I call it aerobics of the brain, and I teach it in workshops.

How should people use astrology? By showing them where there are danger spots so they can take a detour. Good astrology is preventive medicine. I think newspaper astrology columns are too general.

What do people learn at the Iris Saltzman Center? To know themselves through their charts. They have free will to follow it or not. I believe the future is 80 percent destiny and 20 percent free will. I give people tools so they can be their own shrinks. I don't let client use me or any astrologer or psychic as a crutch.

Give an example of a successful reading. A hotel executive who was also into land development was unhappy with his life. He came to me for a reading. I looked at his chart and said: "I see you doing something with medicine or doctors." And he said, "I've never finished high school." But he's now publisher of the main book on alternative medicine!

ASTROLOGER

JOJO SAVARD

JoJo@JoJoSavard.com
(310) 356-0020
1209 Manhattan Ave., Manhattan Beach, CA 90266
www.JoJoSavard.com

For years she's been the most famous astrologer in Canada, but this Manhattan Beach resident now draws charts and speaks all over the US.

www.facebook.com/JoJoHoroscopelady
www.linkedin.com/in/JoJoSavard
www.twitter.com/JoJoSavard

To schedule a phone, Skype or in-person reading go to
www.JoJoSavard.com

Why did you want to put your brother in a closet? When I was only five, I had a vision of my tiny two-year-old brother traveling to heaven by train at his coming birthday. I tried to warn my family to put him in a closet to keep him safe but they thought I was crazy. Tragically, three days later, he was found dead, hit by a train.

Why are you sometimes called "Astrobarbie"? I've been described as a live Barbie doll and a one woman show. When I was a teenager, I was a carnival and beauty queen and won best sets of legs in the neighborhood! At the University, I worked as a model and an aerobic teacher in Gold's gym.

Now I'm older, but who cares? Age is only for wine and cheese. I love pink, high heels, sexy clothing, wild hairdos, splashy flowers, everything glitter, big colorful hats,, and dancing until the wee hours of the morning. Since childhood, I've designed my own avant-garde clothing and living décor for my TV shows, infomercials, and cellular programs—as well as writing many of the scripts! I'm also a painter and have had many art exhibits. You can get a free one-hour Skype reading if you buy one of my paintings. Look out Gucci, Spielberg, Scorsese—and Picasso!!! [See JoJo's Art at http://jojosavard.com/]

You're pretty optimistic aren't you? I believe that that life is perfect and everyone is perfect, and behind the clouds there's always a bright sunshine. There are no problems, only solutions. As children of the great creator, we are small creators, and within our hearts we have the same ability to create miracles in our lives and manifest our wildest dreams.

Describe some of your international successes? I was the first and only life coach/astrologer who had her own weekly and daily astrology TV show on national television—in French and English—for many years across Canada and eastern US. I was on the front page of the famous Canadian magazine MacLean's, the equivalent to *Time* magazine in the U.S. I've been a guest on Jay Leno, David letterman and so many others. I have read for Canadian Prime Minister Jean Chretien, Tony Bennett, Celine Dion, and many others, I had three big lottery winners from numbers I gave them on TV. One was a desperate woman who had lost everything in a bad divorce. I co-created the first personalized astrology audio line, Internet video horoscopes, producing and providing video horoscope shows on mobile phones carriers in the U.S. and Canada.

PALMIST

MARK SELTMAN

MarkSeltman1@gmail.com
(212) 777-0540
111 East 7th St. #72, New York, NY 10009
www.MarkSeltman.com

Mark Seltman has been called "the Mozart of Palm Readers."

www.facebook.com/masterpalmist
www.linkedin.com/pub/mark-seltman/3/119/602
www.twitter.com/MarkSeltman

BOOKS: "Real Palmistry: Your Life is in your Hands."

To schedule a reading, call (212) 777-0540 or
go to www.MarkSeltman.com

How does being a palmist affect your private life? I find myself surreptitiously looking at people's hands wherever I go. Sometimes when I'm on the phone with someone who's not a client, I'll spread the tarot cards to gain additional insight into the conversation, although, I never let anyone know I'm doing that.

Have you had any other careers or interesting jobs before this? As a child, I was an avid musician, performing Chopin on the radio at age seven. I also loved art and won several art awards. Utilizing that talent, I became an industrial designer, inventing dozens of products that were frequently ahead of the time.

As a hobby, I like to recycle and reuse items, reconstituting them into something else that is long-lasting and useful, whether it's a milk or yogurt bottle, or a steel desk someone threw away. I have been called "The Guru of Garbage."

You're called a "Palmist" but do you look at anything other than hands? I use hands for understanding character; astrology for interpreting life cycles, patterns, habits, and timing; and tarot for getting at unconscious issues. Relationships, family dynamics, and career are my specialties.

When did you first realize you had this gift? I don't really consider being an expert palmist a gift, but a skill that I developed over many years of hard work. Any intelligent and intuitive person can read hands if they're willing to do the work.

Have any celebrities or business bigwigs expressed interest in having you read their hands? I have read for Martha Stewart, Star Jones, Cindy Chu, Patti Davis, and dozens at special events such as Katie Couric, Kyra Sedgwick, Kevin Kline, Barbara Corcoran, Dave Brubeck, Maurice Sendak, Marvin Scott, etc. Because of my extensive corporate special event work, I believe that I've read more CEOs, CFOs, CIOs, and COO's than any reader of anything anywhere.

What made you interested in reading hands? Everyone has hands, and they're a topographical map of your character in the past, present, and future. The value of palmistry is in its capacity to quickly identify basic character and behavior.

Do hands change? Yes, they change as a person's thinking and circumstances change. The tiniest change in a line can symbolize a huge change in a life. You can observe your successes and failures reflected in the mirrors of your hands over time.

Why aren't there more respected palmists like you? Unfortunately, modern palmistry is still relegated to the realms of gypsy fortune-telling scams and disreputable storefronts adorned with red neon hands. There's no spokesperson to educate people about it. To this end, I've written "Real Palmistry." My plan is to give everyone a helping hand—their own.

Can someone read their own hands? You can ask your hands questions like: "Who am I?" "What do I value?" "What do I think?" "What's my philosophy?" "How can I be more spiritual?" "What's next?" and more.
Priceless knowledge and insight await you in plain sight at the ends of your arms. Knowing yourself places your free will and destiny exactly where they belong, back in your own hands.

What is a typical session for you? I normally spend 1 ½ - 2 hours with clients. I don't like watching the clock and believe that clock watchers shouldn't go into this career.
I like to know ahead of time what clients want to gain insight into so that I can spend time preparing. It's not always what's asked at first that needs to be addressed. There are few questions I won't ask and many I won't answer. I don't like "What's going to happen?" I never answer "When am I going to die?" I also avoid "yes" and "no" answers.

What is the most unique experience in your life? I once spent two days a week for a two year period helping design a vocational rehabilitation program for 150 murderers and serial killers in a forensic psychiatric hospital in NYC. I got to read many of their hands and hear their stories, which was incredibly fascinating.
Another extraordinary time in my life were the two years I spent as an initiate in the Martinist Order. I participated in miraculous healings, learned to astral project, and practiced unique ways to focus my mind and imagination.

145

Do you predict celebrity romances and breakups? Yes, because stars and fans want to know about their personal lives more than anything! Using astrology, I can predict how compatible a couple are, the challenges they will have and potential breakups. In Hollywood, everybody breaks up so the fun in celebrity predictions is to forecast how many months or years the romance will last! When I read for celebrities, their professional lives are different from ours. But their personal lives are much the same....we all want to find true love.

What type of people are the hardest to help? Men are more cynical and disbelieving than women. I think it's because they work off a different side of the brain than we do!

Do people listen to what you say? Yes, many have taken my advice and made some wonderful life changes financially, professionally and personally. Some people hear what they want to hear though. I was talking one day on the phone with a woman who was cheating with a married man. She wanted to know when he was going to leave his wife to marry her. I told her I didn't see him leaving and that sometimes you have to let the husband and wife work it out for themselves. She left him and soon after found a new guy who was available! The husband and wife are still together.

Do you tell people if you see a dark future? I won't answer the question of "when am I going to die?" That's between you and God. But I do tell people if there is a challenge coming so they can be prepared for, avert it or deal with it. Knowledge is power! I am honest with the client. But my belief is everything happens for a reason and the end result is for the best even if we can't see it at the time.

Who was responsible for your gift? My birth mother, Angie. She was an astrologer/psychic who saw the same talents in me and taught me everything. I was adopted and raised Catholic. I met Angie in my 20's and had nine years with her before she died of breast cancer.

What do you see in your own future? I'm currently touring the country with my soulmate and husband, Joe Lawson, on our *Soulmates and Hot Dates; Past Lives, Present Loves Tour*, that has sold out in major cities. I see us helping more and more people understand their life purpose and special soul connections with others.

147

How did a mistake get you interested in astrology? When I was 12, I saw an ad in a comic book to write away to get a free astrology chart, and they sent it to me. And it was the wrong birthday! But after reading it, I was hooked anyway. I was like a little kid who had never taken piano lessons and sits in front of a piano and can instantly play everything. It was an instinctual memory.

How do you combine being a psychologist with being an astrologer? Before every session, I have a chart in front of me that I draw up before the person comes to see me so I know what their patterns are. It's a shortcut. Most psychologists have the patient tell them a story. I tell them a story. I find a pattern and reframe it to them like "Wait a minute, just because you're a Gemini doesn't mean you…" It's like I'm giving them permission slips. "This is who you are and give up trying to change it but let me help you reframe it as the gift to you that it is." I sit with the client and help them understand their soul from a chart's point of view, reduce the judgment, and have them fall in love with their fate.

Do astrology and psychology go well together? Carl Jung said psychology will be a dinosaur science until it includes astrology. I combined the two first with a masters in clinical psychology from Antioch and additional studies at Harvard and York University in Toronto. As for astrology, I had a radio show at 28 and I've been doing this for 35 years and every day I do five readings so when people say how good I am, I should hope so by now.

What was your most bizarre case? I went to a murderer in prison and helped him understand his violence, His girlfriend was my client, and I gave him compassion for what he had done. Everybody deserves compassion in my map. In his case, he murdered his sister's boyfriend by mistake. She was in the bedroom and screaming and he ran into help and he hadn't intended to kill him. I helped him tell that story.

What do people say on your radio show, "Tell Me a Story." Many of the calls are people telling their secrets and me making it acceptable. Somebody calls in and says they have nowhere to live, they're about to fall off the planet, and somebody will call in and help them. Or someone calls in and says their father just died and we have the ability to give her a wave of compassion.

How does your show help people? If they're feeling bad about themselves, I let them know that "God didn't have a bad day when He made you." I help give them a positive frame of who they are, to reframe a sad negative point of view and help them fall in love with themselves. Everyone should know how to love themselves. I once got myself flowers. And I fall in love with other people all day. I'm a Gemini. I can't help it.

Which celebrities that you've worked with surprised you? I was given to Madonna as a birthday gift to her by Sting and I was in awe. She has an unbelievable level of intelligence. I was blown away by her sincere desire to be an artist. It wasn't coming out of ego as I would have expected. She is completely committed to her art.

Do you tell clients the truth? I am known for being super-duper blunt. So if someone is talking to me and complaining on and on about her husband, I'll say "You've been married to him for 35 years and you're never leaving him so we'll talk about why you're with him."

How do you help your clients with your readings? I can help them break patterns that don't serve them for a long time and they don't know how to break them. They may not know why they're doing what they're doing. I have a lot of compassion. I'm not just an astrologer but a good healer who gets people out of their rut so they end their broken repetitious negative patterns.

How else do you differ from most astrologers? I don't do predictive astrology. I am not interested in when you're going to meet the tall dark handsome man or when you are going to die but when your thought process is ridiculous and how can you change it. I'm not a normal astrologer. I don't talk about Pluto and Neptune. I speak English and I speak straight to your psychology which is interrupting your life, and I change your point of view.

What type of readings do you enjoy most? I like it when people come to me who have fallen out of love and after reading their charts and letting them talk, I help to remind them what they once loved about each other. I take them back to the beginning when they first met and fell in love—and then they fall in love again...

PSYCHIC MEDIUM

ROXANNE ELIZABETH USLEMAN
(212) 588-1797
PO Box 981, New York, New York 10150

www.Roxanne.net

This eclectic psychic medium has been featured extensively in all major media, is a "vintage store psychic," and has also taught the Learning Annex's most popular course on how to attract your soul mate.

BOOKS: "Altered States Of Consciousness: Unleash The Extraordinary Power Of Your Magnificent Mind."
Coming soon: "Soul Mate Secrets 101."

To schedule a phone or in-person reading,
call (212) 588 1797

You teach courses in attracting soul mates. How do you know when you've found one? There is only one soul mate per person, and you can only meet them when you have evolved enough in your life to be in a certain point in your consciousness.

When you do, it's like you've found the other half of your heart that is missing, and you can then have and be more in your life. When that happens, it's a knowing that you're with the right person. It's like a plug into a socket creating energy and light. Some people have "twin soul mates" who they think is their soul mate but isn't. They think they're perfect—until they find their real soul mate. Still, they may learn a lot from that twin relationship.

Are there any people who can't be your soul mate? Yes, those who are already married or in a serious relationship, that's not good karma. Or if they pass away. Or if the other person gets involved with something very bad for them like drugs. Usually soul mates help to bring out the best in each other, so if they're hurting you or pulling you down, that's not your soul mate.

What can people do to find a soul mate? Your soul mate is already planned for you, but you can draw the person in sooner by getting rid of serious blocks first, which could be emotional, spiritual, physical, or mental.

If you've met your soul mate in another lifetime, it would be easier to meet them in this life. Your first step is knowing what a soul mate is. Second is releasing the blocks that you have which keeps you from finding one. And the third is attracting your soul mate, say with Internet dating, or doing new activities, or working with your angels, or traveling. You need to make yourself a more interesting person which opens up the doors to meet more interesting people.

Are there exercises people can do to attract a soul mate? In my book and course, *Soul Mate Secrets 101*, I give people exercises and imagery. You can start by acknowledging a block or a fault or something about yourself that you don't like or have to work on, and that is the first step to change. You can write down where you feel the block started in your life, say from your childhood, or someone you dated, or your parents, or even something you brought in from another lifetime. Writing down things and then looking at them later is good. Another thing is to reflect upon this and what you want before you go to sleep at night because sleep is your inner therapist. Another exercise is to write down 101 qualities that you're looking for in your life partner, which gives you the

152

opportunity to be able to think about what you really want. And then you have to look at yourself to see if someone like that would be attracted to you. You may want someone interesting, but are you interesting enough that they would want you?

Do you also help individual clients to find their soul mate? Yes, if they're doing a reading, and want to know if someone is their soul mate, they show me a photo or their handwriting sample. If they haven't found him/her, a reading can help them.

You're involved in so many interesting things. Describe your work "as a vintage store psychic?" I work with racked.com and curbed.com, two popular fashion sites on the Internet. They've filmed many segments about vintage and antique shops with me. They have me go into the stores, touch the objects and tell who owned them before and what their history is. Objects communicate differently than we do, and I translate so mortal beings can understand it. By touching something, I can tell what happened when the object was worn or owned [Search for "Vintage Store Psychic" at YouTube.]

***The New York Times* and *New York* magazine said you give tenants in certain apartments free readings?** Yes, I work at a very high end Chelsea mansion where tenants pay $15,000 a month rent. And a one-hour reading from me is included when they move in. *New York* magazine wrote: "So far [celebrity psychic Roxanne Usleman] has garnered raves from tenants who have lobbed her questions about everything from careers....to finance...to romance."
I also work with objects in their home to give them information, say they've bought an antique, or they want me to look at the photos hanging in their apartment and learn if they will bring good energy. Plus, I've given very accurate predictions annually on *CNN*, *Fox News* and *Nightline*.

How do you feel about being psychic? The word "psychic" has so many negative associations: the "900-Number" infomercial, the storefront palm reader, the "tell you what you already know, grab your money" charlatan. Yet the true psychic is a person who is especially sensitive to non-physical forces. The psychic is the guide who connects with the higher forces of the mind, and his/her natural gift comes from the creator.

PSYCHIC (SPECIALTY: TAROT)

VOXX

Voxx@Voxx.org
(323) 782-0222
www.VoxxThePsychic.com

Specializing in relationships, Tarot International calls her "The World's Most Accurate Psychic," and she's named a Tarot Certified Grand Master Supreme by the International Tarot Certification Board.

www.facebook.com/Voxx1
www.linkedin.com/pub/voxx-the-psychic/5/874/592
www.twitter.com/Voxx

BOOKS: "Angel Magick," "Goetia Magick: The Lemegenomicon," "Goetia Magick: Spirit Reference Book."

To schedule a phone, Skype or in-person reading, call (323) 782-0222 or go to http://voxxthepsychic.com/services.html

Has your gift helped you or those close to you? Being clairvoyant, clairaudient and clairsentient guides and protects me and my family. It has even saved my life, and loved ones. My Spirit Guide "told" me to break up with a boyfriend, which I did. He was killed in a car accident a month later. I also had a vision that my eldest sister was in danger of being killed by her boyfriend. She kicked him out, and he returned to town a few months later, killing another woman, and her young son.

Do you do crime psychic work? I used to, but I don't enjoy it. Even though I helped exonerate a man unjustly accused of homicide, and solved another case. However, the judge let the murderer go free, and he's still out there. He killed an entire family and got away with it. Doing crime work is terribly sad. I dislike seeing visions of dead children, however they died. Such experiences made me decide to use my psychic gifts to help people plan their best futures, by using their talents.

How old were you when your abilities began to be apparent? At three years old, I could sense what people would say and do beforehand. I began studying astrology and tarot at seven. At that age, I accurately predicted the pregnancy of a family friend, who did not know she was pregnant. I also predicted the gender of her future baby.
Soon, I began seriously studying metaphysics and the occult. I learned to interpret dreams, omens and signs. At twelve years old, a family friend said she'd bought an astrology chart, but didn't understand it. I interpreted it, and she paid me $100. I've been reading tarot and doing astrology for others since then.

Was there a family background in spiritual matters? Yes. I come from an entire family of born psychics, on both sides of my family. On my paternal side, I'm descended from Malcolm III, King of Scotland, in addition to famed occultist, Aleister Crowley. My maternal side contains Italian Strega, and healers. I was born in Ethiopia, growing up all over the world, including Saudi Arabia.

Describe your favorite case. In 1997, I was psychically visited by the spirit of the young rock star, Jeff Buckley. He had recently drowned in a Memphis river, and his body was missing for ten days. In a vision, his spirit showed me what had happened. I sent this info to his family, and his mother verified the accuracy of my vision. Jeff's spirit also told me his exact date and time of birth, so I could do his astrology chart, Info his mother later confirmed that no one else had known.

My favorite celebrity matchmaking case was the marriage of Peter Fonda to one of my clients.

What do you do that makes clients trust you? First, I do not advertise, I feel the universe sends me the people I am meant to meet. Most people contact me because I've been recommended by someone they trust. Also, I only require the person's first name and last initial. This eases the client's mind, knowing they haven't been "googled." They sense that the psychic reading comes from a real place.

You seem to have many gifts. I use a combination of psychic skills with the mastery of astrology, numerology, tarot, and trance mediumship. I get info from the 72 angels of the Qabalah, and channel angels and spirits. I do automatic writing on a computer, with my eyes closed, typing 150 wpm. I also write books, screenplays, music and poetry.

Using these tools, what do you do for your clients? I get to the heart of the matter quickly and accurately, telling it like it is, with compassion. My clients get details, dates and specific names. I use astrology and numerology to obtain dates and details; clairaudience to obtain names; clairvoyance for visual details, and the tarot to insure the info is not just a projection made by the client. I truly get my information from The Creator.

What type of clients do you like best? I can read anyone. I especially enjoy reading for artists, scientists, doctors and inventors. I hope my visions can help such clients accomplish something meaningful for mankind.

Your predictions have gotten you on some major shows. What were they? I've successfully predicted every President since 1980. Years ago, on *The Tonight Show*, I correctly predicted the next two Presidents, (Clinton and Bush), and their double terms. I appeared on *The Jimmy Kimmel Show*, predicting various winning football teams, plus the fact that Jimmy wouldn't be marrying his then-fiancée—totally right on. I appeared on the BBC, publicly channeling the spirit of the late pop star, Michael Jackson. My most famous, documented prediction was the Japanese tsunami, March 11th, 2011, which I accurately predicted three days earlier on my psychic blog.

How did you get known as The Psychics' Psychic® and SuperPsychic®? After I became a professional psychic, my reputation grew and other psychics came to me. One of them called me a psychics' psychic. Then, when I hosted my own live cable show, giving readings to callers, people started saying I was a super psychic. I decided to keep both names.

What is your method? Before clients come to me (or call me, since I have clients around the world) I meditate on them for half an hour. I don't know anything about a first-time client or why a regular client wants to consult me. I write down what I pick up and tell them when the reading starts. Clients often tell me I answer their questions before they ask them.

What are some examples of your work as a medium? While meditating on a first-time client before she arrived, I heard a girl's voice telling me not to throw out her white shag rug and stereo set. When I told the client about this, she was stunned! She said the voice belonged to her daughter who had died recently and she had come to ask me what to do about the white shag rug and stereo. Another time, a client, whose wife had died recently, was consulting me about his business when suddenly his wife arrived uninvited. She came through to scold her husband, "Please stop eating all those bagels with your coffee. You'll stuff up your system and constipate yourself." He complained, "She's still nagging me about that from the other side."

What about your clairvoyance? During a reading for Laura, a woman I'd never met, I picked up a serious medical problem her friend, Jane, had. Jane had a tumor beginning to grow in her uterus. Laura warned Jane about it. Jane's doctor discovered she had the early stages of cancer of the cervix uteri. Her life was saved. I often give readings to people I've never met, but this time I gave a Psychic X-Ray to someone I'd never heard of who wasn't there at all.

What other areas do you work in? I predict Wall Street movements, often to the exact date, with 85 percent accuracy. I also read animals. Once, a horse breeder was desperate because one of her horses was very sick and the vets at the animal hospital said he was going to die within 48 hours. I told her what was wrong with the horse physically and emotionally and how to take care of him. She did what I said. The horse improved immediately and continued to live. My client told me the vets said it was a miracle.

In your book, "The Naked Quack," you warn us that many thousands of psychics are either frauds or incompetents. Why do people go for them? People don't know what to be amazed at! Since no certification or licensing is required to become a professional, anybody can do it. And since there are no standards to judge by, quacks don't have to be gifted, they just have to seem to be. Chances are, millions of people have never gone to a legitimate, gifted psychic but to a quack, who comes off like an expert.

What should you watch out for during a reading? Some psychics ask you questions, questions, questions, then feedback your answers. You're giving yourself a reading! Watch out for psychics who are too vague or hypothetical. The two most popular words of a quack are "if" and "maybe."

Did you study to become a psychic? No. When I was four, I died in a car crash; but I was sent back from the next world and told I'd been given a great gift and an important purpose in life. But I wasn't told what the purpose was.

What did you do before you were a psychic? I was a successful photographer. In New York, I shot parties, headshots, and did corporate photography for Exxon, Clairol, Cuisinart and ad agencies. My art photography was exhibited and won awards. I was certified an Artist by the New York Bureau of Cultural Affairs. Then, as a stringer for Newsweek while living in Europe, I covered the Cannes Film Festival and the Volvo Tennis Open in Monaco. My photo of Princess Grace was published in the Spanish Tenis magazine. My art photography was exhibited in France and Spain, and two prestigious art photography magazines each devoted six-page spreads to my work.

Why did you quit such a successful career? I was giving readings to friends, which was satisfying my soul. My psychic gift was pulling me toward becoming a full-time professional, searching to discover the Purpose in life I was told I had when I was a child in The Next World. My psychic work taught me my Purpose: To use my gift to help people get closer to God.

How difficult was Lifetime TV's *America's Psychic Challenge*? The degree of difficulty of the tests were extreme. Honestly, I did not know that I could accomplish some of these feats such as being taken to a large parking lot and picking the one car that held a man concealed in the trunk. Or remote viewing the Queen Mary. Or without any prior knowledge, I had to give the exact details at different crime scenes.

I was awarded the title of "America's #1 Psychic" after successfully finding a man buried underground in ten acres of desert.

Did your Spirit Guides or Angels help you? Each day before arriving on set, I would pray and ask my angels to walk with me. By following the directions given by them, I was able to prove to the world that there really are gifted psychic mediums.

Did you jump at the chance to enter the contest? When I was first approached, I declined. Twice. The production company's standard contract was horrible: contestants couldn't talk about the show, there was no pay, they wanted to own everyone's lifetime story rights. I was worried since reality TV is a huge risk, the editors can cut the footage as they please and you have zero input. More than six months later, the show came back to me. We renegotiated the contract and my Angels told me to do it. And when my Angels tell me to do something, I must.

Since you had proven yourself by winning this prestigious contest watched by millions, did you stop taking these challenges? Oh no, I am the most tested psychic in the U.S. For example, after *America's Psychic Challenge*, I went on to be tested in the *Global Challenge: Sixth Sense International* which is airing in Europe.

The tests were more intense! The producers blindfolded us to take away our sense of sight. Plus they put each of us in wheelchairs to remove our sense of direction and wheeled us on location.

When did you first realize you had this metaphysical gift? When I was a toddler I could see and communicate with my Guardian Angels. They were my constant companions, protectors, teachers and playmates. This is the reason that I wrote my first children's book, "My Invisible Friends: Angels." It's so important for parents to understand that Guardian Angels can be seen by many children. We all have them; they are assigned to us by God.

How did you get started professionally? From the age of 18 I was a cosmetologist and women were coming to me for advice and beauty treatments. I guess I've always had a sign above my head that said "Get Counseling Here...."

What is your most unusual case? I was called in because a three-year old was having seizures. He was just beginning to talk but it was gibberish. I understood that he was a little medium, and he was hiding from the spirit of a lady that had died in that home.

The ghost was traumatizing him and he was having severe anxiety attacks and seizures. His parents were stunned and once the spirit was removed, the boy was free of his torment, anxiety and the convulsions.

I feel that I excel as a Health Intuitive. I can psychically see and scan the energy field and the physical body to predict and identify medical issues. Since I'm not a doctor, I send clients to the type of specialists they need.

What tools do you use in sessions? Photographs: they capture the very essence of a person's aura. When I look into the eyes, they tell me everything because they are the windows to the soul.

Whom do you like working with best? I love working with children because when you help a child you change the future. I'm also very interested in Indigo children and so many are being born right now. These are highly evolved souls that have come here to help save this planet. These psychic children have indigo blue colored auras and they come here knowing that they have a mission and purpose.

Tell us a few things about your sessions. I find that my phone sessions are just as accurate as in-person ones because I am not getting the information from them but a higher source. I read for all types of people; from the lady next door to investment bankers, producers, deal makers, rock stars, TV stars and even a treasure hunter. Knowledge is power and I'm often used as a secret weapon to get the inside scoop on business deals, family issues, partnerships and lovers too. "Confidentiality" is my middle name.

Because you're such a famous psychic, are people ever uncomfortable with you? Yes, some are afraid that I'll know their dirty little secrets and hide their eyes or shy away from me. But it's a gift to know who has a clean mind, pure spirit and who doesn't.

162

INTUITIVE PSYCHIC

STACY WOLF (JAMES)

StaceyWolfOffice@gmail.com

www.StaceyWolf.com

www.facebook.com/thestaceywolfjamespage
www.linkedin.com/in/staceywolf
twitter.com/StarSignStacey

BOOKS: "Psychic Living," "Never Throw Rice at a Pisces," "Get Psychic," "Secrets of the Sign," "Love Secrets of the Signs."

To schedule a telephone or in-person reading, go to www.Stacey-Wolf.com/consultations.html

You used to be a stand-up comedian. What were some of your favorite psychic jokes? I would choose a guy in the audience and ask: "Do you believe in past lives, sir?" And he'll usually say no. And I'd say, "Well, I see that in your past you could have been my brother. No, wait, maybe it was my sister. I want my dress back. And Mom wants to know why you haven't called her in two hundred years."

Or I told the audience, "I'm such a good psychic I write my diary a week in advance."

Or someone from the audience would shout, "If you're really psychic, what's my name?" And I'd say, "Let me guess. 'Loser'? Do you really want me to guess your name—or what everyone else calls you?"

What's the hardest thing to get used to as a psychic? I have a lot of one-sided conversations with people. I'll see a client and say, "You're getting your hair done tomorrow," or "Your daughter is going to be in the school play." People don't even have to talk back to me. I just know.

How did being a psychic help you when you were younger? When I got older, I always knew exactly what was going to happen throughout the day so I knew what I needed to carry with me. Band-Aids. Nail files. I had it all. My friends were amazed. "You always have everything," they'd say to me. And I'd say, "No, I only have what I'll need."

Were you successful in your career before this? I was an actress, and people may have seen me if they took a Continental Airlines flight years ago. I was the one doing the safety video they showed at takeoff! Before I did that job, I went to work at MTV, but my show was canceled.

What led you to become a professional psychic? After my show was canceled and I was unemployed, I had time on my hands. I went to a tarot reader who was really bad, and I thought, "I can do better than that." With plenty of free time and nothing to do, I studied my new private passion—tarot cards. That was my spiritual awakening.

What's your feeling about doing tarot card readings? People think the cards are doing things, but they're just a laminated deck of cardboard. The universe is putting them into order.

Tarot readers are not all fortune-tellers and Gypsies. They come from a variety of backgrounds and are everyday people, like myself.

Some people think we are doing pretty much the same thing but all readers develop their own way of reading the cards. And it's impossible to have every answer to every question. Tarot card readers are not infallible.

You've been called a "bridal astrologer." Explain. One of my new books is "Never Throw Rice at a Pisces," the first wedding planning guide for brides who like astrology. And speaking of brides, I was lucky enough to be one myself and I married a wonderful man.

How do you feel about past life counseling? If someone asks about their past lives, or wishes to channel wisdom from the divine, or talk to a deceased relative or pet, I do that as well. But I don't believe past lives are ultimate truth, and I always say that in the sessions where this comes up.

You say you help people take off the clothing that doesn't fit. Explain that? Just hearing a voice or seeing the energy around someone and I can immediately identify the core of who they are, what they should be, and what's holding them back from being all they can be. People really change and they are so grateful for the insight, it's immediate and wonderful to see!"

How accurate are you? Many people tell me that whatever I say to them comes true. They'll lose their job, and I tell them that they're going to get an offer for a better job with more money in six weeks that is more managerial and it happens.

We first interviewed you almost 20 years ago. What has happened to you since? Wow! I've been on many TV and radio shows including *The View*, *Beyond with James Van Praagh*—who wrote that I was "one of the most gifted intuitives [he had] ever met"—*Late Night with David Letterman*, and have been written about in *The New York Post*, *Mademoiselle*, and many other magazines and newspapers, most recently, *New York Magazine*.

I have written five books—two psychic and three astrology ones—and I was the astrologer for *Cosmopolitan* for a few years. I've married, I've traveled a lot—and I don't do stand-up comedy anymore!

LYNDA WOOLF

LyndaWoolf8@gmail.com
(775) 315-5558 USA, +65 9832 8295 Singapore

www.LyndaWoolf.com

An internationally acclaimed Intuitive, Healer and Life Coach, she reads and lectures in Singapore and throughout the US, working from her home base of Nevada

To schedule a telephone or in-person reading, call (775) 315-5558 or email lyndawoolf8@gmail.com

You read a lot for people in places like Singapore, and Hong Kong. How does their divination differ from ours? We're more scientific. For example, a friend told me that a master he had visited told him that 90 percent of ghosts in China are tamed by a master, which I don't believe. Chinese psychics may predict people's futures on the basis of phrenology, while I tell the future from a person's energy, which I see. I have learned a lot from Asian and European cultures and blended the different philosophies into one that works in all situations for all people.

Are the questions clients ask the same in Asia the same as here? Over there they often want to check the feng shui of a newly opened restaurant. Or get an auspicious name for a new child, or a name change, because they believe a good name can affect one's future.

Why would they choose a westerner to read for them? Some people are just plain old curious and want to see what the difference is for themselves. In Asian fortune-telling, it is about superstition, and their Gods, and so they are looking for straightforward answers that allow them to take control of their destiny. I am respectful of their beliefs, so I give them a path to navigate that doesn't violate their cultural philosophies.

How did you get your family to accept that you were a psychic? I grew up in the movie business. My whole family was in it including my father who was an award-winning cinematographer. So I grew up on the stages of 20th Century Fox, MGM and Universal.
My parents never quite accepted that a psychic was something they wanted their child to be. So they told everyone that I was a psychologist.
My dad was working on a movie, and the lead actor went up to him and said, "I know your wife loves to go to psychics and I have found a brilliant one. Please give her the name of this psychic." Yes, it was me, and that gave me credibility in my family's eyes.

Are celebrity problems the same as ours? Some are, but others become fixated on something like weight—sometimes not just their own but even their children's! I feel the best advice isn't to assure them that I see them all as perennially thin, but that it might be best for them to focus on becoming more spiritual to find happiness.

Do you find that being a professional psychic gets in the way of your personal life? It is a challenge to find friends who want to be friends just because I am me. I remember once when talking with Demi Moore—I have also read for Dudley Moore, Ben Vereen, Jack Lemmon, Sly Stallone, and many famous people I can't name—and she had said to me the hardest part was that she never knew who wanted to be her friend for just being friends. And she didn't know who wanted to be her friend because she was Demi Moore.

Do you use any tools? I sit and chat with a new client in the beginning so that they can find their comfort zone. Once they have relaxed, I will start off with a piece of information that astounds them. I do that throughout the entire session, and when they leave, they feel as if they have found a new friend who totally understands them. My greatest joy is giving someone the key to their problems.

Do you ask your clients a lot of questions? As a rule, I don't ask any questions. They just sit and listen because too much information gets in the way of what I know.

So first I find out what makes them tick, and then I see what is in store for them, potentially. If they can truly understand themselves, they can control these outside events and use them to their advantage. Unfortunately, some people are in denial and do not want to hear the truth. I find working with them to be like climbing a mountain of ice in bare feet.

You have done some criminal work. What was your first case? I was living at Lake Tahoe at the time and there was a murder that the police were having trouble with. I went to the locality where the murder took place and found myself taking on the emotions and sight of the victim. It was most disturbing and interesting all at the same time.

I could feel the impact of the drugs that the perpetrators had given to the victim. And then at night, they stood him up in the middle of the road and ran him down. I was able to see what the men looked like and the description of the car they were driving.

The police later wanted to know where the information was coming from as they believed that only someone involved in the crime could have the knowledge that was being given to them.

MORE TOP PSYCHICS AND ASTROLOGERS

DEIDRE ABRAMI
Delray angel healer.
www.psychicdeirdre.com,

KIM ALLEN
New York based spiritual astrologer.
www.kimallen.com

JENNIFER ANGEL
Astrologer for the New York Daily News, resident astrologer at Star magazine, she also does pet horoscopes.
www.mistressofastrology.com

ROSEMARY ALTEA
Spiritual medium from
Venice, Florida. www.rosemaryaltea.com

MELISSA BACELAR
LA based animal communicator (pet psychic).
www.celebritypetcommunicator.com (Recommended by Belinda Bentley)

CLAUDIA BADER
Astrologer & psychoanalyst.
www.claudiabader.com (Recommended by Shelley Ackerman)

LAURIE BAUM MSW
Licensed psychotherapist, professional astrologer, and psychic counselor in Encinitas, California. www.lauriebaum.com

TIA BELL
Psychic who was in "The Real Housewives of New Jersey" and had a show on A & E called
"Psychic Tia." www.thecraftbytia.com

LAURIE CAMPBELL
Medium in Irvine, California.
www.lauriecampbell.net

AIDEN CHASE
Healer & Intuitive called
"Hollywood's Healer."
www.aidenchase.com

CHIP COFFEY
Psychic, medium & spiritual
counselor. www.chipcoffey.com

MICKI DAHNE
Miami psychic medium.
https://www.facebook.com/micki.dahne

ALLISON DUBOIS
Medium from Gilbert, Arizona.
www.allisondubois.com (Recommended by Judy Hevenly)

HALLEY ELISE
Empowerment Intuitive from Boca Raton, FL., also works in Broward & Dade
Counties. www.halleyelise.com

JOHN EDWARDS
One of the world's most famous mediums, who starred in the popular series
"Crossing Over." www.johnedward.net

MATTHEW FRASER
Psychic medium from
Boston. www.meetmattfaser.com,

JOANNE GERBER
Psychic medium and spiritual teacher from Boston. www.joannegerber.com

DEBORAH GRAHAM
Psychic who works in Palm Beach and Dade counties.
www.mrsgraham.com

SHELLEE CASTLE HALE
A criminologist and a psychic, living near Seattle.
www.shelleehale.com

ALLISON HAYES
New York/Asheville, NC, psychic rock reader (crystal communication) and #1 psychic in Supernatural magazine. http://therockgirl.com (Recommended by Michelle Whitedove)

KIM KIMILLA
A psychic medium who specializes in love. www.kimlovemuse.com (Recommended by Michelle Whitedove)

JOSEPH LoBRUTTO III
Psychic medium based in West Palm Beach, FL. www.psychicmediumjoseph. com (Recommended by Laura Mendelsohn)

MICHAEL LUTIN
Astrologer. http://michaellutin.com (Recommended by Mark Seltman)

TONY LEGGETT
Spiritual healer.
www.deartony.com

DANIELLE MACKINNNON
Intuitive life coach in MA.
www.daniellemackinnon.com

CHAR MARGOLIS
Psychic medium in the US and Netherlands. www.char.net

KELI MICHAELS
LA psychic reader, medium and Reiki practitioner. www.askkeli.com

SUSAN MILLER
Astrologer whose popular Astrology Zone website offers free horoscopes.
www.astrologyzone.com

SUZANE NORTHRUP
Medium, with grief and bereavement specialty. www.suzanenorthrop.com

ROBERT OHOTTO
Psychospirituality.
www.ohotto.com (Recommended by Colette Baron-Reid)

HILLARY RAIMO
Intuitive. www.hillaryraimo.com
(Recommended by Michelle Whitedove)

LUISA RASIEJ
Pennsylvania psychic known as the Inner Contessa
www.innercontessa.com
(Recommended by Elizabeth Joyce)

JOAN RANQUET
Animal Communicator.
www.joanranquet.com

RAY OF SEDONA
Psychic spiritual reader in Arizona. www.rayofsedona.com,

NOREEN RENIER
Orlando, Florida psychic detective. www.noreenrenier.com

REBECCA ROSEN
Denver medium and author of the best-seller "Awaken the Spirit Within."
www.rebeccarosen.com

PSYCHIC RYAN
Psychic medium and Reiki specialist. www.psychicryan.com

JEFFREY SEELMAN
Wisconsin psychic & specialist in home hauntings. www.starclear.com
(Recommended by Judy Hevenly)

GAIL THACKRAY
Medium.
www.gailthackray.com.

JAMES VAN PRAAGH
One of the world's most famous clairvoyants and spiritual mediums.
www.vanpraagh.com

NOREEN VIRTUE
Angel therapy.
www.angeltherapy.com

DONNA VOLL
Understanding angelic influences.
www.angelstoguideyou.com. (Recommended by Joyce Keller)

JANET WRIGHT
Chicago-based psychic reader and psychic healer. www.janetwrightreadings.com

THE MOST FAMOUS PSYCHIC IN AMERICA IN 2013 WAS...

THERESA CAPUTO

Also, known as "The Long Island Medium," Theresa Caputo is so popular that her TLC show attracted over a million viewers per episode over the past three years. Indeed, it is the most popular recent show of that genre since John Edwards "Crossing Over." While the two shows are similar, many think she comes across as softer.

Theresa really is a Long Islander, born and raised in Hicksville, NY. She's been married to her husband, Larry, for 24 years, and they have two children, Larry, 23, and Victoria, 19. Her other two "babies" are her dogs, Petey and Louie. She is what she presents herself as: a typical Long Island housewife—except for the fact that she talks to the dead.

On her website, she says she began seeing spirits when she was four, which she thought was normal until she became a teenager and the other teens told her it was not. She was a victim of anxiety for many years, and at the suggestion of her mother, went to a famous spiritual healer named Pat Longo. Longo told her that a spirit was trying to communicate with her, and it was causing her anxiety and aliments.

It was because of this that she found out that she could "communicate with spirit" and became a practicing medium. (She's also a certified medium with the prestigious Forever-Family Foundation, which connects science with the afterlife.)

Actually, she was very successful even before her show. She says she started her business "with only a business card and word of mouth recommendations." Even so, she was booked for two years before her program aired, and now she has a three-year waiting list and is not even booking any more clients!

For more, see www.theresacaputo.com

ABOUT THE AUTHORS

PAULETTE COOPER

Paulette Cooper Noble has written 20 books (and over 1,000 articles) spanning a variety of subjects. Her books include *The Scandal of Scientology, The Medical Detectives, 277 Secrets Your Dog Wants You To Know, 277 Secrets Your Cat Wants You To Know*, along with three books on "retail therapy," including *Bargain Shopping in Southeast Florida.*

She and her husband, Paul Noble, wrote a 1996 book (published by Simon & Schuster's Pocket Books) titled *The 100 Top Psychics in America.* A few of the original psychics have been included in this book, but most of those chosen here are new ones. She also writes pet columns for the *Palm Beach Daily News*: "Pet Set" and "Pet Set People."

Paulette has earned seven writing awards (for her books, articles and a play), and is best known for her activism and research as the first person to expose Scientology.

Originally from Belgium, she resides in Palm Beach with her husband, Paul, and their two imperial toy shih tzus, Polo and Peek-a-Boo. *www.PauletteCooper.com*

PAUL NOBLE

Paul Noble is a retired television programming executive for Lifetime, Metromedia and Fox. He serves on the Board of The Palm Beach County Film and Television Commission.

He has won five Emmys, and has produced many major television talk shows. He also takes the photographs for the "Pet Set People" column in the *Palm Beach Daily News*. *www.PaulRNoble.com*

CPSIA information can be obtained at www.ICGtesting.com
Printed in the USA
BVOW05s0620260214

346056BV00011B/371/P